Literature Guide

Should You Buy This Guide?

40% of my YouTube viewers say my videos helped them i
Another 40% said they improved by one grade. That's jus
much more you will learn from the guide.

The more you read, the more you know. The more you know, the easier it is for new knowledge to be remembered, because it links to your existing knowledge. Cognitive scientists have realised that knowing stuff makes you cleverer.*

Most of us have grown up thinking you have to be clever first. But no.

English Literature is 90% knowing stuff. You've read the poems, plays and novels. If you can remember the themes and quotations, you are 90% sorted.

(So obviously I have a section teaching you how to remember quotations).

If you are on a grade 4 now, you really can get to grade 7 with this guide. All you have to do is read it. Take some notes. Use the notes in some essays. Write more essays without the notes, so you remember them.

That's it, that's all there is to it. Commit to knowing stuff. And if you have a bad exam, you'll still move from a grade 4 to a 5, and probably a 6. I'm not making this stuff up – my students do this all the time.

I'll also show you how to write about texts so that you can get grades 6, 7, 8 and 9. Do I believe more than 20% of students are capable of getting grade 7 or more? I know they can. When you get to the end of this guide, you'll know exactly how to improve by two or more grades.

It's also packed full of essays, so you can see exactly what top grades look like, and how to force the examiner to give you top grades.

And you know, if you memorise the content of a few essays, would you be able to use parts of them in the exam? Of course you could.

If you are ready to dramatically improve your grade, read on.

*Search: Professor Robert Bjork, Professor Daniel Willingham or The Learning Scientists to find out more.

These are just some of the students who wrote to me after the 2018 exams.

Although I will teach you how to get grades 7, 8 and 9, don't let that put you off. I want to show you that anyone can improve from a grade 4 to a grade 7 with hard work, and just knowing what is in this guide.

The students below didn't have my guide, because it wasn't published then – they only had my videos.

G W

I got an 8 in literature and 7 in language!! Couldn't have done it without your amazing videos!!!

Zaim Anjum

Last year I got 3 this year I got 7

Sali Sawo

I've been getting 5s all year round. Your videos really helped and I came out with a 7 in Language (I think 116 marks) and a 9 in Literature (got full marks in Paper 1 and 84 in P2). Thank you!

Rue Topaz

I'm dyslexic and was told that I was stupid , my target was a 5 and I achieved a grade 7 (I'm now also taking literature A level)

And your videos really helped me to achieve a grade I didn't think I could ever get.

Rehab Thyab

Even though I was predicted a 7, in my mocks I kept getting 5s and 6s. I only gained some confidence in the exam due to you Mr Salles. Even my friends who got 9s in both English lit and lang all credited you as their main reason for success. I completely agree with this.

I was honestly so worried that I would have to resit the language GCSE but thanks to you I got an 8. In lit I got a 9 which was also aided by your in depth analysis of Macbeth. I am so pleased with my results and I cannot express enough how grateful I am that I stumbled upon your channel.

Steph Lauren

I honestly do not think I could've got my grade without your videos. For the past three years in high school, I and my whole class had been struggling with an English teacher who wasn't really teaching our class and had given up on us by the beginning of year 11.

I hadn't been getting the grades I knew I was capable of and had no idea where I was going wrong. A couple of weeks before our GCSEs, I found your channel and watched the majority of the videos for my books and cluster of poems.

I took some risks in those exams, and fast forward to August, I got a grade 9 in English Lit, and a grade 7 in English Language on GCSE results day. Thank you so much, Mr Salles! couldn't have got my level 9 or level 7 without your videos :))

Elsa Ruuskanen

I went from a grade 6 in Literature to a grade 9! Thank you so much :)

Sanna Iqbal

I used to get 3s and 4s but today I achieved a 6 and 7 thanks to you. ☐

Live Dash

Hi Mr Salles, I was predicted Grade 6 for English Literature, I watched your grade 9 themes video night before I applied it in the exam without even understanding it fully and I got a Grade 9!

Emma W

Predicted a 4, got a 6

Contents

Exam Timings	p 5
How Your Grade is Worked Out	p 7
What the Examiners are Looking For	p 8
My Checklist of How to Write a Literature Essay	p 11
Example of Grade 5 and 6 Essay Writing	p 13
So, What Does a Full Mark Answer Look Like?	p 14
How Should You Structure Your Answer?	p 16
Plan Your Revision Around Themes to Get Top Marks	p 17
How to Plan Your Answer	p 18
How to Memorise Quotations	p 21
How to Choose Quotations so You Get Top Grades	p 21
Problems with Terminology	p 25
Structure and Form	p 27
Write Less, Score More	p 28
Shakespeare Context	p 31
The Big Themes of Shakespeare and the 19th Century Novel (and Poetry!)	p 42
How Might These Themes Work in an Essay?	P 47
Example Shakespeare Essays	p 48
Essay on The Tempest and Caliban	p 48
Essay on Macbeth and the Witches	p 52
Essay on The Merchant of Venice	p 55
The 19th Century	p 58
Charles Dickens	p 58
A Christmas Carol	p 59
How to Revise for a Dickens Exam	p 63
Great Expectations	p 65
Charles Dickens: A Christmas Carol	p 73
Robert Louis Stevenson	p 78

Jekyll and Hyde Essay	p 80
How does Stevenson present Mr Hyde as a frightening character?	p 80
Essay Based on Extract from The Strange Case of Doctor Jekyll and Mr Hyde	p 83
Paper 2	p 88
J B Priestley, Biography and Context	p 88
An Inspector Calls An Essay on Social Class	p 92
An Inspector Calls- 100% Grade 9 response on Eric	p 96
The Curious Incident of the Dog in the Night Time Essay	p 99
Lord of the Flies Essay	p 102
What Should I do Now?	p 105
Romanticism	p 106
William Blake (1757-1827)	p 107
London By Willian Blake	p 108
Percy Bysshe Shelley (1792-1822)	p 118
Ozymandias, by Percy Bysshe Shelley	p 120
Robert Browning (1812-1889)	p 124
Porphyria's Lover, by Robert Browning	p 125
Don't Read This Section Unless You Want Grade 9!	P 131
Critical Theories	p 131
Alfred Lord Tennyson (1809 to 1892)	p 136
The Charge of the Light Brigade, by Alfred Lord Tennyson	p 140
Poetry Exam Tactics	p 146
Compare How the Poets Present the Effects of War in War Photographer and One Other Poem, Using the FOSSE Way	p 148
Compare How the Poets Present the Effects of War in War Photographer and One Other Poem Grade 7	p 152
Grade 6 Version	p 154
Essay: How do the poets present power in Ozymandias and London?	p 156
How to Choose Poems to Compare	p 159

The Unseen Poem	p 161
What Does a Grade 6 Essay Look Like?	p 164
The Unseen Comparison	p 167
Exam Answer to Unseen Comparison	p 168
Grade 6 Answer Unseen Comparison	p 169
Glossary	p 172

Exam Timings

There are usually 1.5 minutes per mark, depending on the exam board you do, and the paper. Work out the number of minutes available. So, in AQA paper 2 there are 92 marks. Then work out the number of minutes available. On this paper, 2 hours and 15 minutes is 135 minutes.

This means you have 1.47 minutes per mark. So, a 30 mark question will take you 30 x 1.47 = 44 minutes. An easy way to work it out if you haven't memorised this in the exam is to calculate it as 1.5, and take off a minute.

Why Does This Matter?

Many students write too little, and they stop early. If you have 44 minutes, you need to use every one of them on that question. Do not move on more than 2 minutes early!

Hard working students have the opposite problem. They haven't finished the question, and run over. Never run over.

This is because the marks at the beginning of the question are easy to get. Students in your year who are so dumb they ask, "Is Shakespeare still alive Miss?" will still score marks at the beginning of the question. The examiners design them that way, as everyone has to sit the same exam.

The first 5 marks can be earned in a couple of sentences, whereas the last 5 marks might take you anywhere from half a page to a page. Don't overrun!

How Your Grade is Worked Out

Every examiner is trained in the mark scheme. They will do their best to give you a mark based on the criteria.

But the mark scheme *never talks about grades*. This is because the government insists that everyone taking the exam in year 11 has to achieve in line with how everyone in year 11 achieved when they were in year 6.

This means that if half the students in the country were marked in the top band by the examiners, the government would not suddenly award them all grades 7, 8 and 9. No, the exam board would still only be allowed to award 17-20% grade 7 and above.

Similarly, if the examiners used the marking criteria, and no-one in the country got into the top band, the government would still require 17% of students to get grade 7 and above.

Crazy? Maybe. But it does give you one massive advantage. If you keep working, when other students don't, you'll just get higher marks than them. If you revise when other students don't, the same will happen.

When two of you are being chased by a lion, you don't have to outrun the lion. You just have to run faster than the person next to you!

Paper 1

What the Examiners are Looking For

The literature exam will test you in two ways.

1. **On what you need to know to be an excellent student of literature texts.**
2. **On what you need to do to write excellent essays.**

The examiners break this down into assessment objectives like this:

AQA Assessment Objectives appear in bold

Edexcel Assessment Objectives appear in italics

AO1

- **Critical, exploratory, conceptualised response to task and whole text**
- **Judicious use of precise references to support interpretation(s)**
- *The response is a cohesive evaluation of the interrelationship of language, form and structure and their effect on the reader.*
- *Relevant subject terminology is integrated and precise.*

AO2

- **Analysis of writer's methods with subject terminology used judiciously**
- **Exploration of effects of writer's methods on the reader**
- *The response is a cohesive evaluation of the interrelationship of language, form and structure and their effect on the reader.*
- *Relevant subject terminology is integrated and precise.*

AO3

- **Exploration of ideas/perspectives/contextual factors shown by specific, detailed links between context/text/task**
- *There is excellent understanding of context, and convincing understanding of the relationship between text and context is integrated into the response.*

AQA only insists on form and structure being analysed for the top level answers, and doesn't put it in any particular assessment objective: "There will be a fine-grained and insightful analysis of language and form and structure".

So far so boring and abstract. Let's break that down into what you have to know and do.

What You Need to Know:

1. The context of the time. This could be limitless. Useful context, however, are facts which you can link to the author's purpose. These would include:

- What the author is known to have done and said in their lifetime, and especially at the time it was written.
- What important historical events were happening at the time the text was written.
- What genre the author chose to write in, and why.
- What kinds of texts contemporary readers (reading at the time) would have been reading.
- What contemporary readers believed about religion, politics, class, culture, society, gender and race.
- The King James Bible, especially Genesis, because every author you study refers to it in their play or novel, and often in their poems too.

As you can see, general knowledge really makes a difference to how you understand literature. It's not just the text you are reading that you need to know, but a good deal of history and Christianity. You're going to have to read.

2. What different genres are: tragedy, comedy, satire, science fiction, detective, sonnet, ballad etc.
3. Subject terminology to write about language techniques: MAD FATHERS CROCH, SOAPAIMS and more.
4. Subject terminology to write about form and structure: act, scene, chapter, exposition, denouement, climax, flashback, volta, sestet, octet, quatrain, couplet, pentameter, iambic, trochaic, contrast, juxtaposition and more.

This guide will take you through all these steps, so that you can write brilliant essays about the texts you are studying. You can be rubbish at this at the start, but will feel much more confident at the end. That's a promise.

Grade 5

Ok, but what if I'm still aiming for grade 5 Mr Salles?

To get 50% of the marks available, you need to do this:

1. Explain in parts (so some parts can fail to explain well)
2. Focus on the full task, everything in the question
3. Make a range of points
4. Choose relevant references (examples and quotations)
5. Link these to your explanations
6. Comment on a range of methods which the writer uses
7. Show how this affects the reader's thoughts and ideas about a character or a theme
8. Use some relevant terminology to discuss literature
9. Explain some relevant contextual factors.

Although grade boundaries change, in 2018 50% in the literature exam would give you a grade 5.

Grade 6

1. **All your explanations are clear**
2. Focus on the full task, everything in the question
3. Make a range of points
4. Choose relevant references (examples and quotations)
5. Link these to your explanations
6. Comment on a range of methods which the writer uses
7. Show how this affects the reader's thoughts and ideas about a character or a theme
8. Use **relevant and appropriate** terminology to discuss literature, with a greater number
9. Explain **several** relevant contextual factors.
10. **Link these to the writer's perspectives and ideas**

In 2018, Grade 6 started at 61%.

So you can see how important it is to your grade to always think about the writer. The very easiest way to write about the author is to make some points about the context.

What was going on in society at the time that made the author include these events, characters, ideas or themes?

If your essay always includes this, you are going to get at least a grade 6. If you do this badly, you'll still get at least a grade 5.

Translation of the Mark Scheme for Grades 7, 8 and 9

AO1

1. A well-structured argument which begins with a thesis.
2. Each paragraph is ordered to build the argument to prove your thesis.
3. Explores at least two interpretations of the character or the author's purpose.
4. You pick really good evidence, or quotations, to back up your argument or interpretations.
5. You write about the full task, which always includes the ending of the text.

AO2

1. Your interpretations of quotations look at individual words and phrases.
2. You sometimes find more than one interpretation of the same quotation.
3. You interpret how the form of the text shapes the way the author wants readers to understand it.
4. You interpret how the structure of the text shapes the way the author wants readers to understand it.

5. You use just the right terminology a student of literature needs to explain ideas.

AO3

   1. You write about more than one interpretation. So your thesis argues why one interpretation is better than another.
   2. You use details from the author's life, or society, or literature at the time to back up your interpretation.
   3. Your conclusion sums up why you have picked one interpretation as more convincing than another. It shows why your thesis is correct.

This advice is relevant to all of the essays you need to write on both papers, apart from the Unseen Poem, where you don't include AO3.

As you can see, the best way to improve as a student of literature is to write essays!

My Checklist of How to Write a Literature Essay

You might find this a more helpful way to think about the mark scheme. The mark scheme outlines the skills you must use. This takes the mark scheme and says, "Ok, but what do I actually have to do?"

I wrote this after my students in my second set achieved grade 9s in their exam. This meant that there were 64 students who were placed in sets above them! I wanted to see, of all the techniques I had taught them, which ones helped them write brilliant essays. So I got their papers back from the exam board.

This is what they did.

1. Begin an introduction linking the words of the question to the writer's purpose.

2. Keep exploring the writer's wider purpose – what does his novel suggest about their society?

3. Always refer to society, as this will always involve the writer's purpose.

4. Use tentative language to show you are exploring interpretations – e.g. "perhaps".

5. Use connectives which tell the examiner (and remind you!) that you are dealing with alternative interpretations: although, however.

6. Embed your quotations within the sentence.

7. Use words such as suggests, implies, emphasise, reveals, conveys etc, instead of 'shows'.

8. Use literary language that students of literature at university would also use.

9. All novels deal in contrast and juxtaposition, or pointing out similarities – use these words.

10. Always quote from the ending and interpret the ending – this is where the author makes their purpose most clear.

11. Write a conclusion which deals with how the author wants us to view or change society.

12. Try to include a quotation in your last sentence.

Example of Grade 5 and 6 Essay Writing

Let's look at part of a student essay on the influence of Lady Macbeth. You'll need to read this part of the scene where she has just received a letter from Macbeth, telling her that he has met three "weird sisters". They told him that he would become Thane of Cawdor, and that he would later become king. Lady Macbeth immediately starts to plot how to kill the king, and decides she'll persuade Macbeth to do it. This is that moment, written as a soliloquy.

The raven himself is hoarse

That croaks the fatal entrance of Duncan

Under my battlements. Come, **you spirits**

That tend on mortal thoughts, **unsex me here**,

And fill me from the crown to the toe top-full

Of direst cruelty. Make thick my blood.

Stop up the access and passage to remorse,

That no compunctious visitings of nature

Shake my fell purpose, nor keep peace between

The effect and it! Come to my woman's breasts,

And take my milk for gall, you ***murd'ring ministers***

Here is an Extract from a Grade 5/6 Essay

This would score at least 17 marks out of 30. Grade 5 starts at 15 marks.

Effective use of references

Lady Macbeth needs to hide her emotions from others and wants to **"stop up the…passage to remorse."** This suggests she feels guilt and **"remorse"** and wants to block these emotions. This would shock Shakespeare's contemporary audience, because she is summoning evil **"spirits"**, who they believed in, to help her convince her husband to kill.

Examiner's Comment

Notice how the student zooms in on individual words to write a detailed explanation. This explanation is at least two sentences long.

Understands the writer's methods

She also tries to be powerful, asking the spirits to make her a man. "Unsex me here" **reveals that she wants to be a man in order to become powerful**. She's demanding and expects the spirits to obey her. **Similarly, she wants Macbeth to kill Duncan as soon as Macbeth tells her about the witches' prophecies. She wants power immediately**.

Examiner's Comment

Although the student doesn't name the methods, using words such as 'reveals' and 'similarly' tells the examiner that she is thinking about how the writer is trying to influence our thoughts.

Understands the writer's ideas

She needs to become male, a different "sex" **because women lacked power in Jacobean times. She needs a man's power to convince Macbeth** to kill Duncan.

Examiner's Comment

Notice how useful context is in showing that you are thinking about the writer's ideas. The word 'Jacobean' will always be relevant in any essay on Macbeth, just as Elizabethan is relevant to any essay on Romeo and Juliet.

Links context to the character

Although contemporary women would also want to be more powerful, **this would shock his Jacobean audience**, because they would never do something as extreme as summon spirits.

Examiner's Comment

Although this is a simple point (it doesn't consider why Shakespeare wants to shock this audience) the references to context show that the student is dealing with a "range" of points, and using "several" contextual references.

So, What Does a Full Mark Answer Look Like?

Here is the same answer on the same extract, improved to hit all the criteria.

Lady Macbeth needs to hide her emotions from her husband, which is why she is calling on supernatural power. This possibly reveals her unconscious realisation of her own **hamartia**: she recognises that she is already feeling "remorse" at the thought of killing Duncan. <u>This **foreshadows** her guilt and descent into madness.</u>

When she calls on "murdering ministers" Shakespeare uses the **ambiguous** meaning of "minister" to reveal her **psychological crisis**. A "minister" acts on behalf of someone in authority. Here Lady Macbeth believes she can control the supernatural powers of evil, who must obey her authority.

However, a "minister" in Jacobean times also meant priest. Here Shakespeare's choice of language reveals that she is going against God, destroying the Great Chain of Being, so that <u>her eventual madness</u> will be seen by Shakespeare's **contemporaries** as God's divine punishment.

This audience would be shocked at the speed with which she turns to evil. This evil is also magnified because she needs the supernatural power of "spirits" to convince Macbeth to murder Duncan. This is a deliberate **allusion** to *Eve, who is tempted by Satan, in the form of a serpent, to persuade Adam to eat the forbidden fruit from The Tree of Knowledge of Good and Evil.* This **allusion** is *made more explicit soon, when she instructs her husband to "look like the innocent flower, but be the serpent under't".* Here Shakespeare equates Lady Macbeth with Eve, whose power destroys mankind's innocence forever, and condemns humanity with Original Sin.

Shakespeare further suggests her oncoming madness through Lady Macbeth's **metaphor**, "stop up the passage to remorse". The "passage" is large, much larger than a door, which suggests her remorse is also great, and *therefore will have the power to turn her to madness after Duncan's murder*. But "passage" also means a transportation, suggesting that "remorse" is already on its way, which also implies the speed with which her "remorse" will arrive.

Key

- **Bold = Language we use to write about literature texts: Terminology**
- *Italics = references to what happens elsewhere in the text: Full Response*
- Underline = context linked to our understanding of the character or ideas

Re-read the essay to see how it deals with more than one interpretation. Go back to the 10 point list of what you need to include, and see how this part of the essay meets it.

How Should You Structure Your Answer?

When the examiners created this exam, their advice was, 'do what you like'! There is no requirement to write 50% about the extract and 50% about the rest of the text. Although the question asks you to start with the extract, there is nothing in the mark scheme to make you do so.

But now the examiners are starting to notice a pattern. Students who don't do well tend to panic about the extract. They stare at it, and are not sure what to write.

So, if you are currently getting grades 2-5 I would advise you not to start with the extract at all. Start with what you know about the play which relates to the question.

If the question was about Lady Macbeth's power and influence, here is a list of examples from elsewhere in the play which you might use:

Lady Macbeth is powerful elsewhere when she:

- Takes back the daggers
- Faints when Macbeth has killed Duncan's grooms
- Takes over at the coronation feast

She is powerless elsewhere when:

- Macbeth keeps her "innocent of the knowledge" of his murderous plans
- They sleep apart – he doesn't know what she says when she sleepwalks
- She sleepwalks, and is powerless to influence her husband, as her soliloquy reveals
- She apparently commits suicide, unable to live with her own guilt

Now Look at the Extract

Now you have thought through, and written about the rest of the play, return to the extract. You'll find things now leap out at you – you'll easily see where she has power, or lacks power, because your brain has already been rehearsing these ideas as you wrote about the play as a whole.

In the examples the exam board give us, students at grades 5 and 6 typically write between two and three sides of A4. If you do less than that, it is likely that you won't have enough examples to make a "range" of points, or have "several" references to context.

However, grade 6 needs you to write about the "full task". The easiest way to do that is to start with the novel or play as a whole.

Now think of the ending – I bet you that at the end of text, your character has changed – they are either more powerful, or less powerful than they were earlier on. This is why it is so important to write about the ending early in your essay. It will force you to get more marks!

The 19th Century Text

Do exactly the same – write about the novel first. Then the extract. Remember, this technique is only one you need to use if you are getting grades 2 – 5.

What About Grades 7, 8 and 9?

If you are already at grade 6 or above, the chances are the extract doesn't present any problems for you.

Because you want to write a "conceptualised" response, you need to think about the character or theme from beginning to end of the text. This will show how the author develops the character or theme over the course of the text, so you will be developing an argument.

Method 1*

1. Write about the character or theme at the beginning of the whole text.
2. Find something that relates to it in the extract.
3. Find something that relates to it from anywhere else in the text.
4. Repeat steps 2 and 3 as many times as your writing speed allows.
5. Write about the ending of the text, and show how the character or theme has finally changed.

*at each point, you will try to include the author's purpose in presenting the character or theme in this way.

Method 2

Do the same as the students who are at grades 2 – 5. A major advantage of this is that you can enter the exam with essays already planned in your head, knowing what you want to write before you see the question.

Let's see what I mean by looking at an essay plan you could have in your head, going in to the Shakespeare paper:

Plan Your Revision Around Themes to Get Top Marks

Example of Themes of Macbeth

1. **The Supernatural**

In your revision, you have decided:

- Whether the witches are real,
- Whether they cause Macbeth's desire for regicide and murder,
- Whether Macbeth's visions are supernatural or his own, causing hallucinations
- Whether Lady Macbeth is a witch, or can command spirits
- Whether Shakespeare believed in witchcraft,
- How he tried to flatter King James's belief in witchcraft.

Notice how this will also prepare you for 50% of an essay on Macbeth, and 30% of an essay on Lady Macbeth, 100% of an essay on The Witches, 90% of an essay on power, 80% of an essay on violence, 30% of an essay on Banquo, 80% of an essay on the role of women, 60% of an essay on lies and deceit, 90% on appearance and reality and so on.

So, the other themes you would need to prepare are:

2. **Power and Kingship**
3. **Women and the Patriarchy**

Then the trick is to turn up in the exam and make these 3 themes fit any question you meet.

Notice that these 3 themes will also answer any question in Romeo and Juliet. In this play the supernatural power is fate. You would look at the many premonitions had by the characters. It will also give you an interesting perspective on Queen Mab, and whether she is real in Mercutio's mind.

'Harry Salles Teaches me How to Cheat Legally'

When my son was 16, he asked me to help him with his English Literature revision. (He ranked all his subjects in order of how interesting they were - English came in ninth place!). This meant he didn't want to revise much, so I said yes, I'd help him, but only if I could film it for my channel. You can see the above named video on *An Inspector Calls*.

In those days, you could take your text into the exam. I know, right. You'll see me asking Harry what quotation he might use to prove his idea. He then shows me the quotations in the back of the book – there are around 6 quotations for each character, which the editor has chosen as the most important.

Harry then tells me what he will do.

He will make those quotations fit the question, no matter what the question is.

That technique works, as does revising with Mr Salles!

It is very easy to dismiss that video now, as you can no longer take the book into the exam. But that misses the point. If your revision says, 'I'm going to make these themes fit any question' or 'I'm going to make these quotations fit any question' you will dramatically boost your grade!

I filmed his total revision for English literature. It took just 4 hours. He scored 99% in his literature GCSE.

So, this technique really works – knowing that you will fit these three themes to any and every question will help you focus in the exam, and dramatically cut back on your revision time.

How to Plan Your Answer

This is a bit like getting dressed in the morning. I could tell you the most efficient way to do this, having researched whether it is quicker to put your shirt on before your trousers (yes) or your socks on before your underwear (no), but that won't help you.

If you already have a routine, my method will slow you down, because you will have to think about it.

The same is true of planning – keep a method that works for you.

But How Do You Know What Works?

Your plan earns you no marks. None! So, it only serves as a very quick pause in which you think about which ideas will get you most marks.

So, no matter what the question, your plan has to include:

- The writer's purpose or purposes
- The key themes
- Then some notes on how to use these to answer the question
- Then some quotations or events which link to these themes

All this has to be done quickly, in no more than 3 minutes, preferably 2.

If you have revised really well, you can do it in under 60 seconds.

To show you how important that is, let me illustrate it with a question.

"How does (insert name of author) create an atmosphere of fear, or mystery, or suspense in (insert name of text)."

Nothing in that question asks you to write about the author's point of view. And nothing asks you to write about the themes. Many excellent students will write the whole essay, saying nothing which will get them into the top band. WTH. As you can see, this makes me really angry.

One way of looking at this is that the exam board expect you to be able to work this out for yourself – if you are good at literature, you will, and get a high mark, and if you are bad at literature, you won't, and your lower mark will be fair.

That is how the exam board look at it.

Another way of looking at it is it stops too many students getting really high marks, so it is easier to find the top 17% who are going to get a grade 7 and above.

Let's apply this question to Jekyll and Hyde.

It's All About the *Why*!

My plan will start with Stevenson's purposes and themes (which are in bold):

1. To entertain a gullible readership.
2. To educate the more intelligent readers about the **hypocrisy of middle class men**.
3. To challenge the **idea of a God**.
4. To allow the gullible readership to read it as a story of God punishing the wicked.

Those are the "why".

So now I try to apply the types of fear to these purposes.

- I can write about Dr Lanyon's fear of a world without God, so that he chooses to die.
- Jekyll's fear of discovery as a hypocrite, with secret desires and habits which would cause a scandal if discovered, so he creates Hyde to live them for him.
- Hyde's fear of death and punishment.
- The reader's fear of scientific discovery, which might suggest the death of God.

- The reader's fear of drug addiction, which is punished in the novel.
- Any sense of fear in the extract, which leads to the reader wondering about any of those things.
- The readers feeling a sense of suspense about what is likely to happen next.

If I don't think about the author's purpose, I am very likely to write mainly about the last bullet point. I will write about **how** fear is presented, but nothing about **why**.

How to Choose Quotations so You Get Top Grades

Quotations are like Top Trumps – you don't need every card in the deck, you just need the ones with awesome power.

Here's how you pick them.

1. Start with the themes, the big picture. These quotations will help you write about the author's purpose and point of view, which will get you the top grades, and also are the point of studying literature in the first place.

Let's say there are 5 themes.

2. Find the best 5 quotations for each theme.

3. Now, some of these are more important than others. Quotations from the end are most important, as these always deal with the writer's final point of view. There has never been an essay title in any exam that couldn't be answered with a quotation from the end of the text. The ending will link to most of the themes and characters.

4. Now allocate those quotations to characters as well. Often you will find one quotation tells you about more than one character.

How to Memorise Quotations

Ok, the key to memory is rehearsal and association (cognitive science tells us this). Google 'The Learning Scientists' for more.

1. Write out the quotation on a revision card.

2. On the other side of the card, write the first and last letter of each word, with the correct spacing for the other letters. Like this:

    Cannon to left of them,

    Cannon to right of them,

    C   nt l to t m,

    C   nt r to t m,

3. Once you have mastered these, blot out the last letter of each word.

4. Write them out with only the first and last letters of each words in the right place. Try this one from Macbeth:
    We hvae sochectrd the sknae, not klield it

5. If you find you are struggling with a pile of quotations which are more difficult to learn, take one and draw a picture to remind you of it. This picture should take you under 30 seconds – you are after an idea you associate with the quotation, not a drawing anyone else would recognise. It's your association which will make it work.

For example, Jekyll describes his first experience of being Hyde as "but not an innocent freedom of the soul". I might draw a red shoe, sitting in a smoothie cup. The shoe might remind me of "soul", red reminds me of a lack of innocence, and the smoothie also reminds me of "innocent", as it is a brand name. Your associations would be completely different. That's the point.

6. But, this is all next to useless if you can't use them. So you need to do brief 5 minute bursts of writing, where you try to include as many of the quotations as you can.

My example from Porphyria's Lover, by Robert Browning (Love and Relationships Poetry Cluster)

Porphyria's **shoulder** is **white** and **bare**, covered in her **yellow hair**. Her lover wound it as a **string, and strangled her**. The weather is pathetic fallacy, with **storm** with **rain**. Her **gloves** are symbolically **soiled**. He killed her because she now **worshipped** him, where before she **scorned** him for being socially inferior. He has overthrown her symbolically, attacking the social hierarchy and Christianity, which is why **God has not said a word**. He deludes himself that she is happy, her dead face is **smiling** and her **blue eyes laughed** because **no pain felt she.**

Notice, I am not trying to write an essay. I'm simply rehearsing basic points, but trying to use as many quotations as I can remember from my cards.

Embedding quotations like this in a paragraph will also teach you how to use them in the exam – you will rehearse the kinds of interpretations you want to make so that when the exam starts, boom, it rushes out, ready, without you having to think much.

And the biggest bonus of this is that I can use just these few quotations to write my whole essay!

Now write this paragraph on a revision card. On one side, highlight the quotations. On the other side, write the paragraph with a gap for each quotation. Test yourself.

How do these help with memory?

1. The number one technique is called **retrieval practice**. This means you have to keep trying to remember something, and you will!

2. **Spaced practice**. Don't keep trying to retrieve the same memory. Try it at gaps of one day, two weeks, three to four weeks. These gaps actually make memories stronger!

3. **Concrete examples**. Relate it to something you already know – that's one reason for the picture you draw.

4. **Dual coding**. Learning something in more than one form – e.g. text with a picture, makes it much more memorable than just as written text. Adding them to a song you already know does the same.

5. **Creating a Schema.** A schema is a mental map. New information makes much more sense when it is linked to old information, on your map. Writing a page using as many quotations as possible will link them all together – these links are the paths, roads, rivers and railways on your map – you'll see how everything fits together. Your mind map, and writing your page of A4 will do that for you.

Example: Romeo and Juliet

For example, when Romeo asks, "what light from yonder window breaks, it is the east, and Juliet is the sun" he describes her beauty, but also how he is hooked into a courtly view of love which may be an artificial pose, or unrealistic and immature.

But it also links to the theme of tragedy – Juliet's "sun" is going to set, it has only a brief life, like her own. The linking of "window breaks" jolts us so we temporarily imagine a broken window, and the language of destruction hints at the destruction of their own lives.

In classical imagery, the male would be represented as "the sun", and the female lover is represented by "the moon". Romeo is upsetting the natural order, by making Juliet the "sun".

This of course is the theme of their marriage – the lovers go against the natural order of arranged marriage.

Does Shakespeare want to point out the natural order needs changing, as it is only a social order that makes men more important than women, and allows parents to choose marriage partners?

Or he is arguing that the social order is natural, that parents are best placed to choose husbands and wives for their children? Does he believe that parents, and more importantly, men, know best?

Example: Dr Jekyll and Mr Hyde

Let's narrow it down. Pick which quotations will count for more than one theme and character. For example, "with ape-like fury, he was trampling his victim under foot and hailing down a storm of blows, under which the bones were audibly shattered and the body jumped upon the roadway. At the horror of these sights and sounds, the maid fainted."

This describes Hyde, in **Jekyll and Hyde**. But you can also use it to discuss the theme of Christianity, the theme of Evil, the theme of Evolution and Science, the context of the Penny Dreadful and Gothic Literature, the theme of Drug Addiction, the character of Jekyll, who has both created Hyde, and kept him imprisoned for the last 12 months, causing this fury…

Ok, now when you do this, you can see that not all quotations are equal! Now you can easily get down to 15-20 key quotations.

Now, because you have worked so hard to make your quotations fit so many themes, you have just revised nearly every question! Having fewer quotations is actually going to make you much better prepared for the exam.

But wait, we're not done.

It is very likely that you will have a long quotation. Now your job is to reduce each quotation to the key words. Above, I'll pick out "with ape-like fury". Now I've done that, I'll write around it single words which will help me, from the longer quotations.

"audibly" and "jumped" will help me show that this is hyperbole, and gothic, and not very believable.

"Fainted" will help me show that women are portrayed as both weak and deceiving.

Having these single word quotations is brilliant, because it means I will have "integrated quotations" as the examiner wants for the higher grades!

You get the idea – choose quotations with the superpower of being linked to more than one character and theme.

5. Once you have done this, find a total of the 5 best quotations from each character.

6. Always pick one from the beginning and one from the end of the text. This will help you write about your character's arc, their journey over the text. Every character in the history of texts has always changed, and exploring why these changes happen gets you top marks. This will give your essay a "conceptualised response".

So, if you have 5 themes, and each theme links to only one character, that means that you need 4 more for each character. If there are 5 main characters, that leaves you with a maximum of 20 quotation for a whole play or novel!

In real life, you will remember more than this, because quotations can be single words. But these are the 20 with superpowers.

Practise using them and memory will take care of itself. So will your top grade!

Problems with Terminology

Every year, the senior examiner's report complains that subject terminology is taught badly in schools. Students simply name every technique they can find – oh look, a simile, a metaphor, some alliteration…There are no marks for this, only for explaining what the purpose of that simile, or metaphor or alliteration is. *How does it affect our understanding of the character, or the author's ideas?*

A much bigger complaint is the naming of parts of speech – noun, verb, adjective, adverb, etc. These don't help you explain any ideas or interpretation, so they score no marks.

More importantly, students often get these wrong, so you probably lose marks, as the examiner forms a subjective impression that you don't really know what you are talking about!

Example of How to Write About Parts of Speech.

Imagine the text, "The young man choked, spluttered, coughed and finally exploded with rage."

Meaningless Terminology

The **verb** "choked" implies how upset the young man is, so that his rage is presented as self-destructive.

This would score exactly the same as:

"Choked" implies how upset the young man is, so that his rage is presented as self-destructive.

This is because the fact that it was a verb did not affect the meaning.

Meaningful Terminology

The writer compresses a list of violent **verbs** in one sentence, in order to convey the young man's escalation of rage, which quickly reaches a climax with "exploded".

Here it is very relevant to the meaning that the list is full of verbs. These clearly make the description violent, and also convey the idea of speed *because they are verbs.*

What Terminology Actually Means

These are the words that a student of literature needs in order to discuss literary texts:

Plays

Scene, setting, entrance, exit, soliloquy, monologue, couplet, iambic pentameter, prop, tension, climax, resolution, stage directions,

All Texts

Symbol, characterisation, personification, metaphor, simile, alliteration, contrast, juxtaposition, allusion, portrayal, repetition, tone, irony, dramatic irony, pathetic fallacy,

Novels

Novella, chapter, rising tension, denouement, resolution, narrative, narrator, omniscient, prose, exposition, flashback, foreshadowing, contemporary,

Poetry

Rhyme, blank verse, trochee, dactyl, iambic pentameter, syllable, half rhyme, enjambement, cesura, couplet, rhythm, song, ballad, sonnet, volta, quatrain, stanza, verse, anaphora,

Words to Explain Meaning

Reveals, portrays, signifies, symbolises, suggests, implies, interpretation, a construct,

Structure and Form

Many students see structure and form as the same thing, so let's get more precise.

Form

The form of a text is really another word for genre, or type.

So the form of a poem might be a monologue, a ballad, a sonnet, blank verse, a song.

The form of a novel is, well, a novel, but also the type of novel – detective, gothic, bildungsroman, crime fiction.

The form of a play, particularly Shakespeare, will be a tragedy, comedy, romance or history play. It could be a morality play, which will link to **An Inspector Calls**.

When you write about form, you are asking this question: *how does this form help the writer present ideas about the character and themes?*

Structure

Structure means the way it is put together. How it begins and ends. What is repeated. What is deliberately left out.

For a poem, it might be written in stanzas, with rhyming couplets, iambic pentameter, dactyls, half rhyme, enjambment, caesura, quatrains, volta.

For a novel, there will be chapters, flashback, setting, dual narrative, contrast and juxtaposition, narrator's viewpoint, exposition, rising tension, a chronological sequence, gaps in time.

For a play there will be acts, scenes, entrances and exits, silences, stage directions, plot and subplot, the unities or lack of them, settings.

When you write about structure, you are asking this question: *how does this structure try to control what we think or expect about a character or theme?*

Write Less, Score More

You've probably all been taught a variation of **PEE**, **PEA**, and **PEEL** as a way to structure your paragraphs. If you haven't,

P stands for the **Point** you want to make.

E stands for your **Evidence**, usually a quotation.

E stands for **Explanation**, where you explain how your **Evidence** proves your **Point**.

Teachers then notice that your paragraphs might only have a basic explanation, so they explain you have to *'write a lot about a little'*. Adding **A**, for **Analysis**, is a way round that. Another is to add **EL**, which stands for a second **Explanation** and the **L** stands for a comment on **Language**.

All this is very logical, and certainly means that you can train your writing to get to grade 5 and 6 and, if you write quickly, grade 7.

But it also leads to several problems:

1. Each paragraph has many more sentences than it really needs.
2. Your paragraphs become really long
3. You end up writing about very few quotations or references, so your analysis feels incomplete.
4. You don't have time to write a proper essay, which begins with a thesis, moves through different interpretations and ends with a conclusion which evaluates why one interpretation is better than another.

This means it is almost impossible to get grades 8 and 9, and very difficult to get grade 7.

So, think of **PEE** paragraphs as stabalisers on a bicycle. They help you cycle, but you don't really know how to ride a bike till you take them off.

Lose the Stabalisers and Stop the Waffle

1. Write in PEE sentences, rather than PEE paragraphs
2. Don't worry about the order of PEE
3. Get rid of repeated ideas or words
4. Choose a different word to replace more than one word
5. You don't need to keep spelling out the name of the text

PEE Sentences

Once you have written your essay, it is now time to start getting rid of as much of it as you can, without losing the meaning.

Below you'll find the beginning of a grade 9 essay written by a viewer. Unfortunately, the essay was over 1600 words long – brilliant for his revision, but impossible to write in a 45 minute exam.

I've separated his paragraphs, and tried to write each one as a single sentence. (When you practise this you don't have to limit it to one sentence, but you do want to go through the 6 steps above. You won't be able to get rid of as many words as I do straight away, but you'll get better and better until you find it happens naturally the *first* time you write, rather than when you edit).

How do the poets present the effects of war in 'Remains' and 'War Photographer'?

Introduction to Remains

In '**Remains**', Armitage presents the effects of war in that it creates an inner turmoil for the soldier who is the narrator in the poem, which describes the theme of guilt that war can bring to a soldier, affecting them. **40 words**

PEE Sentence Redraft

Armitage's narrator reveals the guilt soldiers feel in war. **9 words**

Introduction to War Photographer

In '**War Photographer**', Duffy also shows the effects of war on the people involved, as the photographer feels emotionally detached during war and a sense of anger is expressed because of the fact that the general public **do not fully understand** the effects of war. **45 words**

PEE Sentence Redraft

Duffy's photographer feels emotionally detached during war, but angry at the public's misunderstanding of war's effects on its participants. **19 words**

Paragraph One

The soldier in Armitage's poem, '**Remains**', experiences a feeling of guilt and this is established in the second stanza with the repetition of 'three' and 'all'. By doing this the soldier in the poem is trying to ensure that the reader of this poem knows that it was not just him who murdered this man but he keeps trying to shift the blame and regurgitate the fact that it was a group killing because he is guilty and this hints at his inner turmoil. **PEE Paragraph, 85 words**

PEE Sentence Redraft

Armitage's soldier emphasises his group's decision to kill, repeating "three" and "all" to shift the blame to others, but this attempt hints at his inner turmoil. **PEE sentence 26 words**

Paragraph 2

Armitage brings the idea early on that war and the violence that soldiers are exposed can be disturbing. This is contrasted with the end of the poem where the soldier says that he holds the man 'in my [his] bloody hands', the use of the pronoun 'my' instead of 'we' can suggest that the soldier no longer feels as if there is a collective responsibility and feels he is fully to blame - the use of these first person pronouns make it seem as if the poem is becoming a confession. **PEE Paragraph 91 words**

PEE Sentence Redraft

In contrast, by the end of the poem, this initial turmoil is replaced by the soldier's full acceptance of blame, confessing he held the looter's life "in my bloody hands", so the pronoun "my" emphasises his shift from collective responsibility. **PEE Sentence 40 words**

Why This Will Get You Grades 7, 8 and 9

Total of original: 261 words. For many students this will be half an essay and you have only written about 2 quotations!

Your whole essay will have only 4 quotations. It is very hard to be 'detailed' or 'convincing' with such little evidence.

Total of PEE sentences: 94 words. This means I can now write under 500 words, but still analyse 10 quotations. That's a massive difference! I'll always be 'detailed' and 'convincing'. Because I have enough evidence to build an argument and look at more than one interpretation, I am very likely to be 'conceptualised'.

Remember, I haven't got any more understanding of the text. I haven't learned any more literature.

But becoming a better writer has made me a much better student, and earned me a higher mark. If you think about it, this skill will help you with any GCSE or A level which involves lots of writing, not to mention your degree or your job.

Shakespeare Context

Why do We Care About Context?

This section will teach you much more than you 'need' to know about Shakespeare and his time. But knowledge is like owning a car. Yes, it is just a car. But, it allows me to go to work, give my children lifts, teach them how to drive, visit my friends, go to a less crowded gym, work in a school 50 miles away, drive to Europe, listen to audiobooks, charge my phone etc. In other words, it allows me to make many more connections, and to do things I never thought about when I bought the car. It is actually also pretty fun. Knowledge is like that. Once you know stuff, you find ways it connects to all sorts of other stuff, and when you start making those connections is when you have fun.

Context is the car which will allow you to tour through literature. Well, go with me here.

How Should You Use Context?

You should only use context like an embedded quotation. In other words, it has to be linked to your interpretation of a character or theme. In the paragraphs that follow, I'll keep using the context to offer you interpretations **of *Hamlet, Macbeth, Romeo and Juliet, Twelfth Night, The Tempest***

Shakespeare's Marriage

Shakespeare married his wife, Anne Hathaway, when he was 18 years old. She was 26. She was also 3 months pregnant with his child. Think about this in relation to ***Romeo and Juliet***. First, it hints at his experience of forbidden love, which echoes the rebellion of Romeo and Juliet against their parents' wishes.

Next, we have to consider that he is clearly sexually active at a time when virginity, for a woman at any rate, is considered a requirement of marriage. How likely is it that Anne Hathaway had remained a virgin until the age of 26? So, we can read **Romeo and Juliet** as a criticism of the controlling influence of parents, a control that was clearly not placed on him. The whole idea of arranged marriage might seem ridiculous to him.

Or we might argue the opposite. If she did seduce him, how likely is it that the pregnancy was planned, and Ann Hathaway trapped him into marriage? Yes, it is possible that the marriage was arranged in common law, before the church wedding. But it is also possible that the families forced him into marriage because of the pregnancy. We might then infer Shakespeare attacked arranged marriage in **Romeo and Juliet** because he is the victim of it.

The Patriarchal Society of Elizabethan and Jacobean England

Now, let's consider the subservient role of women in the patriarchal society of the day. Yes, women were considered the property of their husbands by law, but what did that mean in everyday life? Is it likely that the 17 or 18 year old Shakespeare seduced Anne, or is it more likely that she took the initiative?

If Shakespeare Loved Anne

When we think this way, we can clearly see why he would write parts for clever, passionate, powerful women, like Lady Macbeth. We might infer that he did not see women as weaker or inferior beings, but men's equal in many respects. And Anne herself would be an odd choice for a highly intelligent, articulate teenager to marry, unless she too were also quick witted and able to keep up with his agile mind.

Moreover, Shakespeare was born during the reign of Queen Elizabeth I, a symbol of women's power and intelligence. We can infer, if we choose, that Shakespeare's female leads are a celebration of their intelligence, rather than a warning to husbands that they need to control their wives. In this reading, Lady Macbeth is not a sexist creation to prove that women are manipulative and evil.

The tragedy of **Romeo and Juliet** would have been avoided right at the beginning if Rosaline had accepted Romeo. Significantly, he is first attracted to Rosaline, who is older than he is, and too mature to believe that Romeo is in love with her, believing instead that he is only interested in sex: she won't "ope' her lap to saint seducing gold". If only Romeo had not tried to buy her affections with gifts, and if only Rosaline did not have to remain a virgin, they might have had a relationship like Shakespeare's.

Seen from this perspective, Romeo's and Juliet's youth and immaturity causes the tragedy.

If Shakespeare Didn't Love Anne

On the other hand, if we believe that Shakespeare's marriage was forced on him, we might argue that Lady Macbeth represents the manipulation of his wife. How likely is it that a 26 year old would get pregnant by accident? How desperate would she be for a baby and a husband in an age where women's status is determined entirely by who they marry? How desperate would she be to have a child when the average life expectancy was 35, because so many children died young?

We might choose to see the trajectory of Macbeth's marriage, starting as equals with "my dearest partner in greatness" to Macbeth's unemotional reaction to her suicide, "she should have died hereafter", to mirror his own marriage.

Shakespeare's resentment can be inferred from his will, "I gyve unto my wief my second best bed with the furniture", which many critics see as a deliberate insult to his wife.

The Value of Friendship in Shakespeare's Life

Shakespeare's first child was called Susanna, and his next children were twins, named Judith and Hamnet. Both appear to have been named after close friends. Hamnet Sadler, a baker, and his wife Judith who were both witness to his will. Shakespeare drew the will up aged 52, four weeks before he died. We can infer from this that Shakespeare believed strongly in loyalty and friendship.

Viewed this way, Macbeth's killing of Banquo is unforgiveable, and much more likely to damage Macbeth than the much more socially damaging regicide of Duncan. This helps explain why Macbeth doesn't see Duncan's ghost, he sees only Banquo's ghost.

It also gives us a critical point of view about Prospero, who buys Ariel's loyalty, forcing Ariel to be his servant for 11 years. Shakespeare would disapprove.

However, we might also use it to sympathise with Prospero's desire for revenge, having been betrayed by his own brother, Sebastian.

Similarly, we might infer that he would expect us to be critical of the Nurse's loyalty to 13 year old Juliet, helping her to arrange her marriage to Romeo. He might expect far greater loyalty to be shown to the Capulet parents who have employed her and trusted her with their daughter.

The Death of Shakespeare's Son, Hamnet

Hamnet died at the age of 11, in 1596. Many scholars wonder what effect this had on Shakespeare's writing. They look to the plot of **Twelfth Night**, where Viola believes her twin brother has died, and to his most famous tragedy of **Hamlet.** The death of Hamlet's father causes him to have a breakdown of identity, and become a murderer, who also drives his lover to suicide.

We might also look at the grief endured by Macbeth and Lady Macbeth at the death of their child. The only reason for Shakespeare to include this as a plot device is to help explain their sudden lurch towards killing.

It might also explain their overwhelming desire for the status of being king and queen, to replace the overwhelming sense of loss they feel.

The tragedy of the play could still happen without any reference to their child's death. We all believe the tragedy begins with his first meeting with the witches. But if Shakespeare wanted us to assume it was simply the influence of their evil, supernatural power, he would have excluded his child's death.

Introducing this death gives Macbeth and Lady Macbeth psychological reasons for their desperate desires. Similarly, if Shakespeare simply wanted to portray Lady Macbeth as evil, he would exclude the detail of her child's death. We can clearly see how their grief is partly responsible for both their tragedies. So then we can also speculate that this may be a reflection of Shakespeare's own grief at the death of son, Hamnet.

Was Shakespeare a Catholic?

There is a good deal of speculation that Shakespeare might have been Catholic. It was illegal to worship as a Catholic in his lifetime, but Richard Davies, the Archdeacon of Lichfield, who knew Shakespeare, wrote that he was a Catholic. We might use this to look at the plot of

Macbeth. Shakespeare creates a 'tyrant king' which acts as a warning of the dangers of tyranny and repression.

This explains Act IV Scene 3, which is usually heavily cut in performance (and possibly by your teacher when you read the play!) Why was it so important to Shakespeare to have Malcolm pretend to be worse than Macbeth? The whole scene is totally unnecessary to the plot – we simply need to see Macduff's reaction to his family's death, which sets up his grief and need for revenge.

Here's some of what Malcolm pretends he will do as king:

"were I king,
I should cut off the nobles for their lands,
Desire his jewels and this other's house:
And my more-having would be as a sauce
To make me hunger more; that I should forge
Quarrels unjust against the good and loyal,
Destroying them for wealth."

Macbeth was written to be performed at the court of King James. He is the main audience, and then the nobles at court, not theatre goers.

Therefore, we might see it as a lesson, played out in front of King James, in an effort to persuade him not to persecute Catholic families following The Gunpowder Plot. This scene is asking him not to take their lands and titles, and not use the plot as an excuse to become a violent, Machiavellian* king.

Next, we might ask how much self-interest there is in this advice, if many of Shakespeare's friends and some of his family are also Catholic.

*Learn this brilliant word. It means using clever, cunning but often dishonest methods that deceive people so that you can win power or control.

Was Shakespeare Homosexual?

Many critics believe that the gender swapping roles of so many of his plays, such as **Twelfth Night**, and his portrayal of powerful women, such as Lady Macbeth, and her demand, "unsex me here", can be explained with Shakespeare being homosexual.

Likewise, many of his sonnets were love poems written about, and apparently to, men. It is impossible to know, but fun to speculate.

He himself had only three children, two of whom were twins. Contrast this to Shakespeare's mother, who had six children, with no twins. This suggests a lack of a sexual relationship with Anne after their first years of marriage.

There were no more children once Shakespeare moved to London to write plays and perform in them, and even though he must have returned frequently to Stratford, having more children appears not to have been a priority for him.

Scholars have long puzzled over the significance of his will, in which he gave his considerable property to his daughter, Susanna, mentioning Anne in the will only once: "I gyve unto my wief my second best bed with the furniture". We might argue that this distance could be explained by his homosexuality, and this would also explain why he had children so young, while still deciding on his sexual identity.

We might use this to look at the ultra-masculine behaviour of Macbeth as a warrior and see masculinity itself as his hamartia. Lady Macbeth perceives masculinity to mean "cruelty" and a lack of "remorse". Both of these allow men to be incredibly single minded and purposeful.

"unsex me here,

And fill me from the crown to the toe top-full

Of direst cruelty! make thick my blood;

Stop up the access and passage to remorse,

That no compunctious visitings of nature

Shake my fell purpose, nor keep peace between

The effect and it! Come to my woman's breasts,

And take my milk for gall".

Giving this view of masculinity to Lady Macbeth could be a way for Shakespeare to highlight what is wrong with his society's view of how men should behave.

Romeo and Juliet: Masculinity and Homosexuality

A good game to play with **Romeo and Juliet** is the "what if?" game. Go through the turning points in the play and ask "what if?" they hadn't happened.

- What if Juliet weren't a Capulet – would they have still fallen in love?
- What if the Nurse had gone straight to Lord and Lady Capulet and told them of Juliet's plan to marry Romeo?
- What if Romeo had not killed Tybalt? Would Capulet have told Paris to keep waiting, and so not forced Juliet's fake death?

When you ask yourself lots of these, you decide for yourself what the most important causes of the tragedy are.

If we look at it from the point of view about social attitudes to masculinity, and to homosexuality, we get lots of interesting ideas.

Act 1 Scene 1 and Rape

Can we argue that Verona's celebration of masculinity as violent and powerful has caused the feud between the families? Romeo's reaction to it feels like a criticism of masculinity: "O brawling love! O loving hate!" The oxymorons suggest how wrong this ideal of violent masculinity is.

It also explains why Shakespeare opens the play, not with the fight itself, but with the psychology of male behaviour.

In a society which values male violence (which both the Montagues and Capulets do), men celebrate violence towards women:

"and therefore women, being the weaker vessels,
are ever thrust to the wall: therefore I will push
Montague's men from the wall, and thrust his maids
to the wall."

Here Sampson celebrates an image of mass rape of Montague women. Shakespeare begins the scene with this and much more sexual imagery as comedy.

So we can interpret this as Shakespeare's criticism of how his patriarchal society dismisses women. The proof of how damaging this masculine stereotype is, is how rape is treated as comedy here.

He could be arguing that laughing about rape is the same instinct that allows fathers to treat their daughters as possessions. Starting the play in this way could be his way of showing his audience that their laughter is wrong, and that the patriarchal society must change.

Why Sampson?

We might also infer Shakespeare's deliberate choice of name, giving these words to "Sampson", the strongest man who has ever lived (Look up the book of 'Judges' in The Bible if you don't know about the biblical Sampson. We first meet him sleeping with "an harlot", a prostitute). He may be making the point that this view of women as objects who simply service male sexual desire is inevitable once society celebrates male power.

We might also ask, what if Romeo had never killed Tybalt?

Romeo tries to avoid fighting Tybalt. If he had succeeded, the marriage would have remained secret, Paris would have to wait "two more summers" by which time peace might have been brokered between the families. Juliet would not have had to take the Friar's potion to feign death, etc etc.

So what drives Mercutio to fight with Tybalt?

"TYBALT

Mercutio, thou consort'st with Romeo,--

MERCUTIO

Consort! what, dost thou make us minstrels?"

The subtext of Tybalt's language is that he is accusing Mercutio of homosexuality. A minstrel is a singer, an entertainer, and easily associated with femininity, rather than powerful, violent masculinity. This invites Mercutio to defend his masculinity. Baz Luhrman uses this in his film adaptation to suggest that Mercutio is actually homosexual, and in love with Romeo. His need to keep this secret, in a society which rejects homosexuality, leads him to fight Tybalt.

In any event, Romeo's explanation of why he doesn't want to fight are easily misinterpreted by Tybalt as a homosexual taunt:

"But love thee better than thou canst devise,
Till thou shalt know the reason of my love".

To Tybalt, Romeo has replied to Tybalt's homosexual taunt in an unexpected way, by declaring a homosexual desire for Tybalt. A basic paraphrase would be, 'I can't fight you Tybalt, because I love you in ways which I can't explain here, but I will show you later how much I love you.'

We might argue that Tybalt becomes enraged because he feels threatened by Romeo's homosexual desire for him. Romeo, of course, has no homosexual desire at all, and "the reason" is simply that they are now related by marriage.

But Shakespeare's point might very well be that the tragedy would not have occurred if men did not see homosexuality as incompatible with being masculine.

King James was homosexual

If Shakespeare were homosexual, it might also explain the popularity of his plays with King James. James became the patron of his acting company, so Shakespeare renamed them The King's Players, and they performed frequently at court.

King James financed the first English translation of The Bible, The King James Bible. In 1611, the year of Shakespeare's 46th birthday, Psalm 46 has "shake" as the 46th word, and "spear" as the 46th word from the end. Many critics believe this is a coded birthday message to Shakespeare.

Macbeth as a coded message to King James

This would certainly help us assume that Macbeth might also contain coded messages to King James.

Shakespeare might well have written the play to show the Court the dangers of a king who was too masculine. Part of his motive might be to persuade the Court to accept James, as an openly homosexual king.

Although homosexuality was frowned on in society, King James was quite open about his homosexual affairs. In 1617 he told The House of Lords why he was honouring his lover with the title, Earl of Buckingham: "I, James, am neither a god nor an angel, but a man like any other. Therefore I act like a man and confess to loving those dear to me more than other men. You may be sure that I love the Earl of Buckingham more than anyone else, and more than you who are here assembled. I wish to speak in my own behalf and not to have it thought to be a defect, for Jesus Christ did the same, and therefore I cannot be blamed. Christ had John, and I have George."

Perhaps part of Shakespeare's motive is to make society at Court more accepting of their new king's sexuality. Perhaps James's patronage of Shakespeare is partly based on their shared sexuality.

Shakespeare the Businessman, rather than an Artist

Shakespeare was also a fantastic businessman. Poems were considered the most worthy kind of literature, and no one had yet written a novel. Books were factual, mainly about history.

So, Shakespeare did not write plays as an artist. When we think of literature we imagine a writer drafting and redrafting until the final masterpiece is published. Shakespeare didn't have time for that – the public wanted new plays quickly.

You might think, Shakespeare is our most famous writer. Surely he was the most dedicated to his art?

Yes, and no. We can read Prospero, a part written when Shakespeare is retiring from acting and writing plays in London, as a celebration of "art":

"And like the baseless fabric of this vision,

The cloud-capped towers, the gorgeous palaces,

The solemn temples, the great globe itself—

Yea, all which it inherit—shall dissolve,

And like this insubstantial pageant faded,

Leave not a rack behind. We are such stuff

As dreams are made on".

However, the same quotation might also be used to show that Shakespeare feels this art is transient, not built to last, and therefore not really important. He may well not have expected his plays to last. Even his theatre, The Globe, was burned down, and he had to rebuild it.

Another fact which suggested he didn't value his plays as art is that he didn't write down the text of his plays to hand on in his will to his family – the plays were instead recreated from memory by actors in his company after Shakespeare's death.

This is incredible when we think about it. If Shakespeare had decided the plays themselves were valuable, as good art always has been, he would have kept copies to be published.

Yes, he did publish 18 in his lifetime, but they were not big earners. He made much more money from his poetry, which were bound in book form. His plays were simply printed on folded paper, called Folios, because they were not made to last.

We can use this information to argue that Shakespeare was incredibly interested in the context of his time. His main impulse was probably to give the audience what they want. Whatever the concerns of the people at the time, and their worries about the politics, war and nobles of the time, would be quickly reflected in his plays.

Understanding Macbeth's psychology is no more important than understanding the fear of regicide, or traitorous Catholics. Understanding Romeo and Juliet's love for each other is no more important than Shakespeare advertising his skills as a writer of sonnets.

Shakespeare, the Sonnet Master

You know that Romeo and Juliet share a sonnet:

"ROMEO

[To JULIET] If I profane with my unworthiest hand
This holy shrine, the gentle fine is this:
My lips, two blushing pilgrims, ready stand
To smooth that rough touch with a tender kiss.

JULIET

Good pilgrim, you do wrong your hand too much,
Which mannerly devotion shows in this;
For saints have hands that pilgrims' hands do touch,
And palm to palm is holy palmers' kiss.

ROMEO

Have not saints lips, and holy palmers too?

JULIET

Ay, pilgrim, lips that they must use in prayer.

ROMEO

O, then, dear saint, let lips do what hands do;
They pray, grant thou, lest faith turn to despair.

JULIET

Saints do not move, though grant for prayers' sake.

ROMEO

Then move not, while my prayer's effect I take.
Thus from my lips, by yours, my sin is purged.

JULIET

Then have my lips the sin that they have took.

ROMEO

Sin from thy lips? O trespass sweetly urged!
Give me my sin again.

JULIET

You kiss by the book."

But did you know Shakespeare couldn't rely on his theatres remaining open? In 1593 and 1594 theatres were closed because of the plague. In later years, performances were banned if there had been more than 30 deaths in London from plague in one day. At these times, Shakespeare made his living writing poetry for rich patrons, and would sell the longer ones as books.

Knowing this, we might question the apparent expression of true love in Romeo and Juliet's sonnet, and ask how much it is actually a reflection of their sexual desire. It sounds like love, but is actually a series of manoeuvres to make sure they have physical contact and then kiss. Shakespeare uses the same skill to manoeuvre what looks like a love poem into an advert for his services as a poet.

It's the idea of the sonnet having more than its obvious purpose which makes us ask what the true purpose of the two teenagers are. We can quite easily infer that parents in Shakespeare's audience would see only hormonally induced passion and rebellion here, and not true love at all.

They might see the teenagers' use of Christian imagery in order to justify their physical seduction as scandalous.

So we might conclude that what mattered most to Shakespeare was money and property, both of which he left behind. Even his actors didn't realise the value of his plays until years after his death in 1616, publishing 36 in 1623, as The First Folio.

Did Shakespeare Write to Make Money?

Several times a term, students will tell me that every writer's purpose was to make money. Usually this is not true. Writers tend to write about a passion, often working at other jobs to make money.

But if we go back before the twentieth century, many writers did see themselves as 'smiths' and 'wrights', old Anglo Saxon words which mean maker and worker. They were wordsmiths and playwrights.

There were 20 theatres in London with a population less than 200,000. This is the size of my home town, Swindon, which has only one theatre! So theatre was 20 times more popular than it is now.

Now, a play at the Royal Shakespeare Company in Stratford will last around 4 months. In Shakespeare's time the play would be performed just once within two weeks. Then it would be on a rotation with loads of other plays, so it might play once every two weeks for a couple of months, or maybe a year.

No one knows for sure, but what is very clear is that plays were not an art form, they were an entertainment and Shakespeare made his money by getting bums on seats. To do that, he had to churn out new plays. So in Shakespeare's case, his purpose really was to make money.

This is still a pretty dumb answer in an essay though. The trick is to explain how what he wrote or portrayed in the play would have appealed to the thoughts, imaginations, feelings, ideas, fashions, concerns and politics at the time. This would then make sure customers paid to come through the doors.

It is probably for this reason that his gravestone ignored his writing, and instead showed symbols of his wealth. Instead of holding a quill, his original grave showed him holding a bag of grain, to represent prosperity and wealth.

The Big Themes of Shakespeare and the 19th Century Novel (and Poetry!)

1. Christian morality and the nature of God
2. Fate and free will
3. Social hierarchy, from the Great Chain of Being, the nobility, to the middle and working classes
4. Education and the rise of the meritocracy as a way to rise in the social hierarchy
5. The role of women in the patriarchy

Using any of what follows in the context part of your essays will propel you to grades 7, 8 and 9.

Knowing this stuff will force you to think about interesting interpretations. You will also have a much more developed thesis to present at the beginning of the essay.

(By the way, these are also all relevant to the extracts you will get in your language papers – they will always have at least one of those themes!)

1. Christian Morality and the Nature of God

God created Adam and Eve in Eden. He forbade them "to eat of the fruit of the Tree of Knowledge of Good and Evil." Satan, in the form of a serpent, tempted Eve to eat the fruit. She was filled with knowledge, and persuaded Adam to eat also.

Because of this, women are traditionally presented as temptresses, luring their men to do things they know they shouldn't do. (This is why Lady Macbeth persuades Macbeth to kill Duncan, and why it is Juliet who makes Romeo believe that he can only be "satisfied" through marriage, which is the cause of their deaths).

God punished Adam and Eve by banishing them from Eden. (This is why Macbeth and Lady Macbeth never enjoy being king and queen, and why Romeo is banished by the Prince, and why Juliet can't face a life without him).

We are all marked by this crime of Adam and Eve against God. It is called **Original Sin**. This means we are all born evil, and must continually strive to be good. (That's why Jekyll creates Hyde, why The Friar tries to end the feud, why Banquo tries not to get involved in Macbeth's plan, why The Weird Sisters don't actually tell Macbeth to kill anyone, why Pip doesn't want anything to do with Magwitch, why The Duke and Porphyria's lover kill their wife and lover respectively, why Jane Eyre doesn't marry Rochester until he is blinded and damaged, and so on.)

By the 19th Century, society is trying to develop different methods of dealing with sin, such as prisons, transportation to Australia and madhouses. There is a growing belief that men can overcome their naturally evil state, and so the death penalty is kept for a shrinking number of crimes.

2. Fate and Free Will

God created Eden as an experiment. He created Adam and Eve "in his image". He was prepared for them to live forever, like God, and planted a tree in Eden called "The Tree of Life" whose fruit would make them immortal.

The experiment was in free will.

Could Adam and Eve refuse to be tempted? The answer is no.

They freely chose to go against his command. However, he continually allows all men and women to exercise free will for the rest of their lives. Only by choosing to live good lives, and make moral choices, can they get back to the state of perfection they had in Eden, and get into Heaven.

We can clearly see this idea of temptation and free will being played out in the choices Romeo and Juliet make about marriage, the choices the Macbeths make about murder, Caliban's desire to rape Miranda, Prospero's desire for revenge…etc.

However, theatre and tragedy come to us from the Greeks, whose civilisation predated Christianity. Greek Gods didn't create a moral universe in which you would get to heaven by being good. Instead, everyone died and went to the underworld, Hades.

Instead, they demanded that you worship them with sacrifices, in order to stop the Gods punishing you in some way with bad harvest, shipwreck, disease, etc. However, the Gods decided on your fate – how and when you would die, and many of the events in your life. In Greek tragedy a character will find out their fate from a prophecy. They try to avoid their fate, but then whatever they do brings about that fate without them knowing it. They can't escape it.

We can see this in the "star crossed lovers" of Romeo and Juliet, and Macbeth's belief in the witches' prophecies.

By the 19th Century, fate is no longer dictated by God, but by social class and education. Although you were born into the circumstances of your parents and family, you could escape it by making good, moral choices, and choosing to better yourself through education and good habits. Characters in the 19th century believe they can change their destinies, and authors in particular make this a fundamental theme of their plots. All of Dickens' plots are like this, and so are Jane Austin's.

3. Social Hierarchy and Class, from the Great Chain of Being, the Nobility, to the Middle and Working Classes

The Great Chain of Being was a way of keeping power with the rich, and stopping those lower down the social ladder asking for more.

The idea was God sat at the top of this chain, then came angels, then the Pope, then kings and queens, then the nobility in all their ranks, then the middle classes (people with wealth but no title), tradesmen, and workers.

In medieval times this meant that God decided on everyone's station in life, and where you sat in the social hierarchy. It meant that kings and queens were appointed by God, by "Divine Right", so rebelling against a monarch was a sin against God.

But this also meant that if you were born into a poor family, well, that was pretty much the way it was supposed to be, and you had to respect the lords and ladies who ruled over you.

Constant plagues and exploration of the new world in Elizabethan times meant this belief was being challenged. Suddenly London expands quite rapidly, it is filled with new businesses, where men can now change their status. Shakespeare is one typical example, starting as an actor, becoming the country's most successful playwright, but also a really successful businessman and property owner.

The idea of people becoming who they want to be, rather than who they are destined to be by birth, is revolutionary.

It is no coincidence that Shakespeare invented the soliloquy at this time (although the Greeks got there 2000 years before). Before that, in Britain, the idea that characters had rich inner lives, and were powerful individuals never found its way on stage. But now that many more people could succeed as individuals, it made sense to show this on stage.

The translation of the **King James Bible** was also revolutionary in this. Suddenly people were able to read the **Bible** and understand its teaching themselves. They didn't have to learn Latin to do it, or depend on priests to explain it to them.

The other attack on the Great Chain of Being is that it was mainly a Catholic idea. Once Henry the Eighth converted to Protestantism, and destroyed the monasteries, this 'natural' order looked less certain. The Pope disappeared from it straight away!

This of course led to persecution of Catholics, and to the gunpowder plot of 1605, which wouldn't just kill King James, but all the nobility in Parliament as well. This is (almost) the first time that a plot against a king had not been led by other nobles, who thought that God had chosen them to be king.

4. Education and the Rise of the Meritocracy as a way to Rise in the Social Hierarchy

In 1800, only the children of the rich went to school. Usually they were educated at home by a governess, (a live in nanny and teacher). Jayne Eyre is such a governess. If they were male, they would then go to a private school from the age of 10. Girls continued to learn at home.

Sunday schools began in the early 1800s, teaching children to read and write, so that they could understand the Bible.

The idea spread, so that Ragged Schools were created to educate the children of poor families. Even so, there were only about 350 of these in the country by 1870.

Workhouses and the Church also set up schools, as did Parishes (equivalent to the council). These all opened schools in order to teach those who could not afford private education.

So, throughout the 1800s, the vision of schooling was to improve the lives of the poor and the working classes. It literally transformed society. Novels and short stories in magazines became one of the most popular entertainments, because they were cheap, and suddenly millions of people could read.

Free Public Libraries were invented in 1850. Although most councils could not afford to fund them entirely, the rich businessmen of Victorian families often saw it as a public duty to fund them themselves.

The growth in industry and Empire led to a huge increase in the number of people on higher income. The middle classes wanted to buy a better education, so dozens of public schools opened to mirror the great public schools of Harrow, Eton and Rugby.

By the 1850s, the idea that girls should also benefit from a private education also took hold, and Cheltenham Ladies College was the first.

In 1870 the government recognised having an education transformed people's lives. Schooling became compulsory and councils had to open schools if there weren't enough to take in children who lived in their area. It was the birth of teacher training, and gradually the school leaving age went up to 11!

In 1891, for the first time in history, schooling had to be offered for free.

This huge growth in literacy and education fuelled the Victorian belief in self-betterment, the idea that anyone can improve their circumstances in life.

You'll see this in any 19th century novel you study. Jekyll is obsessed with doing good works, even while Hyde is living out his secret and shameful desires. However, even Hyde is able to operate as a functioning member of society, being able to read and write, as though this is a God-given right.

Schooling is a central theme in **Jayne Eyre** and **Great Expectations** and the poems of William Blake. Even Romeo comments on the purpose of schooling:

"Love goes toward love as schoolboys from their books,/ But love from love, toward school with heavy looks."

We could read this as Shakespeare's criticism of the boredom of school. Or it could tell his audience what an idiot Romeo is - first he wasted his learning, and now he is going to waste his chance at life.

5. The Role of Women in the Patriarchy

(**Patriarchy** – a society controlled by men, in their own interests, so that women have limited rights and are subservient to males in the form of fathers, husbands, even brothers).

As you know, Shakespeare married a 26 year old Anne Hathaway when he was only 18, and she was pregnant. He was no stranger to powerful women.

His plays are also full of them.

In his society, women were subservient to men. They were not even allowed to act on stage, their parts being played by young men.

In marriage, a woman was literally her husband's possession, and all that she owned became his. This remained true until the 1870s!

With the rich, a father paid a dowry to a suitably rich husband. Marriage for love was a romantic ideal largely ignored by wealthy families, who arranged marriages with other wealthy families. It was therefore very common for rich men to have a mistress, women they had actually chosen for themselves.

Women achieved their status through marriage, and the status of their husband. Within the marriage, their status was maintained in the skill of managing the servants and staff of the house, and often the budget.

Women were not allowed to own property, unless their husband died. But, as a widow, they were expected to remarry. Single women tended to live with their parents, no matter how old they were. When their parents died, they would not inherit unless she had no brothers.

The legal age for marriage was only raised to 16 in 1929!

Added to that, a woman was expected to remain a virgin until marriage. Once married, they might expect to give birth every two years, with an average of 8 children. 30% of these would die by the age of 15.

As you can see, in Elizabethan England, women had few rights, and their main role was as mothers.

This was also true in Victorian England, so that only unmarried women could become teachers. Once married, they had to resign. The expectation was that they would have children which, as you can see, was a full time job.

In Victorian cities, child mortality rates were even worse. Overcrowding and pollution led to a greater spread of disease.

When we study Shakespeare we can see the tension between what society expects from the female characters, and what they want for themselves.

Juliet's desire to choose her own husband. Lady Macbeth's desire for status. The reactions of Lady Macbeth, the Nurse and Lady Capulet to losing their own children.

It is quite easy to see Shakespeare asking for women to have greater power and status in his plays, attacking society's beliefs.

It is also easy to argue the opposite! When we see the women's tragic fates, we can argue this is caused by Shakespeare's beliefs, agreeing with the society he lives in, punishing women for breaking the patriarchal rules.

Personally, I feel he is a champion of women. In Elizabethan England, just as in Victorian England, this championing of women's rights is even more likely given that the monarchs are both women.

Writers in Victorian times are even more likely to champion women's causes. They would still be seen as sexist today, because they weren't campaigning for complete equality. But you will get into the top band exploring how far they are championing the rights of women in their texts.

How Might These Themes Work in an Essay?

Think of context like an embedded quotation. It is a piece of evidence you give *to back up a point you are making*.

However, the biggest benefit to you is in writing your thesis.

Thesis for Macbeth

Shakespeare presents Macbeth as a tragic hero in order to explore the self-destructive nature of a patriarchal society, to serve as a warning to the nobility against the crime of regicide, and flatter King James in to maintaining the social order without persecuting Catholics.

Thesis for Romeo and Juliet

Shakespeare presents the tragedy of Romeo and Juliet's love to warn parents of the need to arrange their children's marriages, while advising them against the dangers of treating women as property and glorifying masculine power. He tries to change the patriarchal society from within.

Thesis for Jekyll and Hyde

Stevenson presents Jekyll's tragedy as a consequence of the hypocrisy of middle class men and the destruction of outdated moral values caused by drugs, advances in science and an understanding of evolution. He argues that Victorian society is so corrupt that it will destroy itself.

To fully follow everything in these you'll need to watch my videos. I'm not expecting you to do that, or understand everything I've written. What I do want you to understand is how you can write a pretty detailed thesis once you understand **the 5 big ideas**.

Having more than one of these in your thesis will force you to argue more than one viewpoint in your essay, and force the examiner to consider whether it is worth a grade 7.

Example Shakespeare Essays

You should read these essays, even if you have never read the plays.

The examiner comment will help you see exactly what the student is doing to get the marks. ***This is different from what the student knows about the play.***

By not knowing the play, you can focus on the student's skills, so you can do what this student does.

Look out for the bold vocabulary – this is where the essay uses subject terminology. (These are words, remember, that you would use in any literature essay, or specialised vocabulary to discuss specific genres).

Essay on The Tempest and Caliban

How does Shakespeare present Caliban's determination, to claim what is rightfully his?

Shakespeare **presents** Caliban's determination to claim what is rightfully his as **ambiguous**. Shakespeare's **presentation** of Caliban is dependent upon how we choose to **view** Caliban and Prospero's treatment of him.

Caliban can be **viewed** through many different **interpretations**: to some he may be a victim of misplaced trust, unjust servitude and theft of his birth right. To others, he is an attempted rapist, 'born' evil and manipulative. To many, he is somewhere in-between; although he tried to rape Miranda, was he acting on animal instincts; has he ever been taught the difference between right and wrong?

If we **view** Caliban as a **victim of oppression**, we have more **sympathy** for his desire to claim back the island, which he proclaims is 'mine by Sycorax my mother'.

Examiner Comment
Here the student outlines her thesis as a question. She knows that presenting the question as two different interpretations will inevitably hit the criteria of AO1 below.

Caliban is **presented** as trusting and somewhat vulnerable. He **instinctively** trusts Prospero as he 'showed thee all the qualities o'th'isle'. Raised without a father figure, Caliban begins to **view** Prospero as father like, so he 'loved' Prospero. Just as Prospero is Miranda's 'schoolmaster', he attempts to educate Caliban. This may suggest that Prospero began to **view** Caliban as one of the family also.

Further suggesting Prospero's affection, Caliban reminisces to when 'Thou strok'st me and made much of me'. The word 'strok'st' suggests that Prospero nurtured Caliban and treated him kindly.

Examiner Comment
These two paragraphs offer a detailed interpretation with embedded quotations. She zooms in on individual words in the quotations. Because she looks at the character over time, she is implicitly writing about the structure of the play. These all meet AO2.

Alternatively, 'strok'st' could also suggest that Prospero **viewed** him as a glorified pet; Prospero never **viewed** him as fully human. **Thus**, when Caliban attempts 'to violate/The honour of my child', Prospero labels him as a 'monster'. As opposed to educating him, he withdraws all fatherly affections and becomes his 'master'.

Although Caliban clearly attempted to 'violate' Miranda, perhaps he was merely acting on his animal instinct to 'peopled else/This isle with Calibans'. The word 'peopled' suggests that his drive was an evolutionary one: reproduction. Rape is a human **concept**, so if Caliban isn't fully human perhaps he just needs to be 'taught' these **social etiquettes** and does not deserve to be imprisoned. This **interpretation** of Caliban encourages **sympathy** towards his situation and determination to reclaim his 'isle'.

Examiner Comment
These two paragraphs offer a detailed alternative interpretation of Caliban, using the same evidence. This therefore meets AO1 and AO2 in much greater depth.

Although Prospero may have been unwilling to teach Caliban social values, one **reading of the play implies** that Prospero 'taught' Caliban cruelty. When plotting to murder Prospero, Caliban uses brutal and threatening language similar to Prospero's. He proclaims that he will 'Batter his skull, or paunch him with a stake'. This can be seen in act 1 scene 2 as Prospero using violence to make Caliban do as 'I command', threatening to 'Fill all thy bones with aches, make thee roar'. Both the words 'batter' and 'roar' create particularly violent **imagery***. 'Roar' could also be a **reference** to Caliban's un-human like **qualities** and the 'monster' that Prospero claims him to be.

Additionally, Caliban refers to 'my dam's god Setebos'. Interestingly, he does not refer to 'Setebos' as his own god, nor is 'god' capitalised, suggesting that he does not affiliate with the devil. This would suggest that Caliban was not 'born' evil. He then suggests that Prospero 'would control…Sebetos'. Perhaps Caliban believes that Prospero is the greater of two evils, which in turn, suggests that Prospero 'taught' him cruelty and 'evil'. This **interpretation** ridicules Prospero and supports Caliban as rightful owner of the isle.

Examiner Comment

These two paragraphs again show so many of the skills of AO1 and AO2. She now starts to examine the world of the play, particularly in her analysis of the island's gods. This is a sophisticated interpretation of the context within the play, and meets the criteria of AO3.

We also get a sense that she is building a thesis which is more sympathetic to Caliban than to Prospero.

notice that "batter" and "roar" are both **verbs, but she doesn't tell us this because knowing they are verbs adds nothing to her interpretation. It is irrelevant terminology.*

Further contradicting the idea that Caliban is 'a born devil' is the **poetic language** he uses to describe the 'isle' with 'sounds and sweet airs…Sometimes a thousand twanging instruments'. The use of **sibilance** to **describe** the 'sounds and sweet airs' creates a soft tone and **reflects** that softer side of Caliban's **temperament**. He notes the 'twanging instruments' suggesting that he has an appreciation for the romantic 'sounds' of 'nature' which fill his 'isle'. This kind-hearted appreciation of beauty and nature may indicate Caliban's true self: before he was corrupted by the language of Prospero. **Moreover**, his appreciation for the 'ilse's' natural beauty, presents him as the worthy and rightful owner of the 'isle'.

Examiner Comment

*Although there have been numerous examples of subject terminology so far for AO2, the analysis of sibilance makes it easy for the examiner. This is because she doesn't just spot the feature, **she explains how it affects our understanding of the character of Caliban**.*

On the other hand, Shakespeare also **presents** Caliban as **evil and manipulative**. When Caliban drinks with Stephano and Trinculo, Caliban appears quite intoxicated. He is almost speechless, offering only to 'lick thy shoe' in an attempt to become Trinculo and Stephano's servant.

However Caliban, when unravelling his plot to assassinate Prospero, appears to give orders in **iambic pentameter form** in: 'Having first seized his books, or with a log/Batter his skull'. If Caliban was truly drunk he would not have been able to give orders so clearly (true to **iambic pentameter** form and in **blank verse**). This **demonstrates** that Caliban, like Prospero, can be **manipulative** as he takes advantage of Stephano's and Trinculo's drunken state.

He also understands that to 'burn' Prospero's 'books' will render him powerless and he will be easier to overthrow. As Stephano and Trinculo have no magical powers and are 'drunkards', perhaps Caliban anticipates that they too will be easy to overthrow, in order for Caliban to gain back the island. **This presentation as calculating and manipulative** makes us **less sympathetic** towards his determination to claim back his 'isle'. **However notably**, Shakespeare often only allows noble **characters** to speak in **iambic pentameter**. This would suggest that Shakespeare views Caliban's pursuit of the island as a noble pursuit. This is perhaps confirmed when the island is left to him as the play ends, and the humans return to Italy.

Examiner Comment

The exploration of iambic pentameter and blank verse indicating Caliban's status is an examination of the play's form. This now meets all the criteria of AO2. One analysis of form is enough to get the grade.

In conclusion, Shakespeare presents Caliban's determination to gain back the isle as a worthy and just pursuit. **Although** Caliban **can be viewed as manipulative** and a 'born' devil, his **initial** hospitality towards Prospero suggests an **innate** kind- hearted nature before Prospero taught him cruelty and pain. In this way Shakespeare supports Caliban's **quest** to regain control of the isle.

What Should I do With That?!

- Pick the Shakespeare play you have studied.
- Now write about a character or theme, using every word in bold in this essay. You will learn how this subject terminology will dramatically improve your grade.
- For extra marks, try to write it with the same number of paragraphs.
- Then tick off how many of the skills below your answer hits. If you do it badly, you'll still have most of grade 7!

Grades 7, 8 and 9

AO1

1. A well-structured argument which begins with a thesis.
2. Each paragraph is ordered to build the argument to prove your thesis.
3. Explores at least two interpretations of the character or the author's purpose.
4. You pick really good evidence, or quotations, to back up your argument or interpretations.
5. You write about the full task, which always includes the ending of the text.

AO2

1. Your interpretations of quotations look at individual words and phrases.
2. You sometimes find more than one interpretation of the same quotation.
3. You interpret how the form of the text shapes the way the author wants readers to understand it.
4. You interpret how the structure of the text shapes the way the author wants readers to understand it.
5. You use just the right terminology a student of literature needs to explain ideas.

AO3

1. You write about more than one interpretation. So your thesis argues why one interpretation is better than another.
2. You use details from the author's life, or society, or literature at the time to back up your interpretation.
3. Your conclusion sums up why you have picked one interpretation as more convincing than another. It shows why your thesis is correct.

As you can see, the answer meets all the criteria, and would consequently score 30/30.

Essay on Macbeth and the Witches

"I'd appreciate if you could skim through my work and tell me roughly what level I'm at and how I could improve. I think I went a bit over the top with esoteric language rather than actually analysing the text. Keep up the great work :)"

This is a great essay written by a generous viewer, Joel Braun. Thanks Joel.

Shakespeare uses the witches in Macbeth to give a form to the **abstract concepts** of temptation, through **religious symbolism** and **imagery, embodying** the deeply **powerful forces** which govern mankind. The **transient** and fleeting **influence** of temptation is also **demonstrated, portraying the limitations of power, echoing Christian sentiments** of good's triumph over evil.

Examiner Comment

This is a very ambitious thesis, and reminds the examiner that this essay should contain several different interpretations. This will score highly in AO1 and 2, and has already anchored the examiner's thoughts to giving you a high grade.

The witches are a **personification** of the **temptation of sin**, and **thus** possess the power to play upon the **protagonist's psyche** and pathological **desire**. The play begins with the unholy trinity of "thunder", "lightning" and "rain". **Thus,** the witches are **symbolically** fused with the superstitious evil **associated** with these chaotic natural occurrences. To an **Elizabethan audience**, these natural **phenomena** would have been inexorable and unpredictable.

This portrays the **power** of the witches. They, like weather, have palpable **influence** over man. This torrential **imagery** is also a **metaphor** for the **psyche**; implying the **forces that govern** the mind are **powerful** like the weather, and that the **protagonists** may fall victim to **psychological** storms.

Examiner Comment

There is a danger of getting lost in a Thesaurus here. However, the candidate is still offering interpretations. He has linked this to the contemporary context. Linking the turbulent weather to the storm facing the psyche is sophisticated, and can be viewed as an analysis of structure.

This is shown through Macbeth's intense deliberation in Act 1 Scene 3, and Lady Macbeth's guilt and eventual death. These **can all be argued to be consequences** of the witches on multiple levels of **analysis**; the prophecy of the witches **could be seen to be** what sparked Macbeth and Lady Macbeth to commit regicide. **Symbolically**, the sin of their action would be inseparable from the **symbolic association** with Original Sin, the intrinsic sin and evil of **the human condition**.

However, the power of the witches is also shown to be **transient** in nature. They themselves are only seen in passing, and disappear as soon as they come; "the earth hath bubbles…and these are of them". This **motif** of disappearing as soon as they appear is reflected throughout all aspects of the witches and portrays the futility of their power.

Macbeth, under their influence, is spurred by the witches. He sees his position fall just as quickly as he had attained it. This aligns with the **Christian** sentiments which Shakespeare was conveying such as **divine justice**; the **fate** of the witches is to be lacking power over nature itself, but they can temporarily bend it until it snaps back into place.

This is also portrayed through the short length of the play; Macbeth is the shortest play that Shakespeare wrote, in conjunction with its circular narrative which resolves the play in a way parallel to its beginning shows the witches to merely be a "bubble" in the final analysis.

Examiner Comment

The first paragraph is a sophisticated analysis of the play's structure, and the second links this to the play's Christian context. This meets the criteria of all the assessment objectives. The third paragraph is an interesting idea which is not fully backed up with evidence. Marks are not taken away for this!

The supernatural lack the power to directly kill, as is shown through Act 1, Sc 3 where the witches stir up a tempest so that Macbeth would sleep "neither night nor day". While explicitly, this would seem to indicate a lack of power, they indirectly have power over people due to the powerful influence they have on the conditions which shape someone's actions. This sentiment of sleep being ruined by the witches is echoed when Macbeth hears a voice "Macbeth doth murder sleep"; here it is shown that to "murder sleep" is more pathological than it may seem, to murder "sleep" results in true bloodshed. This indirect control over man would be deeply disturbing to the Elizabethan audience, where witchcraft was feared.

Examiner Comment

This is a sophisticated comparison of one theme over different sections of the play, and therefore leads to a conceptualised analysis of language, structure and context.

In conclusion, the witches do possess power over nature and the future, through twisting falsehoods into true prophecy, capable of using mere suggestion to tear down the tragic hero Macbeth, and throw all of Scotland into chaos. But, despite their power, the storm they cause inevitably passes, and the tyranny they inflict on the world is dissolved. Thus, the divine order of nature is always maintained, with the witches eternally being of an inferior strength to mother nature herself.

612 Words

Examiner Comment

Most student will need at least 700 words to develop a strong enough argument to merit grades 8 or 9.

However, if we look back at all the bullet points in the assessment objectives, we find that each one has been dealt with. This would therefore be marked at the top of the mark scheme, with 28, 29, or 30 marks. Different examiners will react differently to the length.

The high quality of vocabulary will also influence many or most to overlook the brevity of the response. Quality vocabulary inevitably prevents waffle, and leads to shorter essays.

What Should I do With That?!

Do the same as last time!

Essay on The Merchant of Venice

How does Shakespeare present Shylock's feelings about the way he is treated?

Shakespeare **presents** Shylock's feelings about the way he is treated in a number of ways. Shakespeare makes it abundantly clear to the **audience**, who at the time were most likely **Christian**, that Shylock's most **defining characteristic**, is that he is Jewish. This is **highlighted** by the **stage directions**, when Shylock first enters the stage: 'enter Bassanio with Shylock the Jew'.

Examiner's Comment

This is a clear statement. However, it does not look at Shakespeare's own point view – is he supporting society's racism or asking his audience to challenge it? Is he arguing that Christianity should be tolerant of other religions? Is he campaigning for religious tolerance as a way of suggesting that Protestants should be more tolerant of Catholics? Once you have an answer to these, you can present a thesis which will lead to a conceptualised response.

Shylock's feelings about the way he is treated as a Jew become clear when Antonio and Bassanio approach him for 'moneys'. Shylock reminds the men of how they have treated him 'and for these courtesies' should he 'lend' them 'moneys'? He has been persecuted for his religious faith, had 'spit upon' his 'Jewish gaberdine' and 'rheum upon' his 'beard'.

Both the 'gaberdine' and the 'beard' **symbolise** the Jewish faith. Shylock is suggesting that the Christian men have mocked his religion by spitting on **aspects of his identity** which are a 'badge' of his faith. Shylock even suggests that the men have called him a 'misbeliever'. This implies that if you are not of Christian faith, your faith is worthless, wrong. **However, despite** this abuse, Shylock has 'borne it with a patient shrug'. The **phrase** 'patient shrug' suggests that he has not risen to their cruelty, that he does not dwell on their 'courtesies'.

Examiner's Comment

This is a very in depth analysis of Shylock's character. But it treats him as though he is a real person, saying 'this is what he is like'. Instead, the analysis should consider Shylock as a construct, asking 'why has Shakespeare presented him in this way?'

As the play progresses Shakespeare **portrays** a change in Shylock's outlook, from a 'shrug' to actively seeking 'revenge'. The first time in the play that Shylock suggests he is serious about his 'bond', seems to come as a direct response to his conversation with Salarino and Solanio. They mock Shylock for his 'daughter's flight', admitting that they aided the elopement of Shylock's 'own flesh and blood'. It is clear to them that Shylock is upset with the disappearance of his daughter, yet they 'laughed at' his 'losses'. This use of alliteration further emphasises the cruelty of Christian men towards Shylock.

Examiner's Comment

The essay now hints that Shakespeare is critical of the Christians' racism, but the point could be made more explicitly by dealing with characters as constructs.

Furthermore, the men metaphorically state that 'there is more difference between' the 'flesh' and 'blood' of Shylock and Jessica, than there is between the quality of wine in 'red wine and Rhenish' (a common wine). Here they are suggesting that Jessica is innately **superior** to Shylock because she has run away with a Christian man and converted to Christianity. Shylock reacts to these unkind words by threatening to take his 'bond' from Antonio. This suggests that for Shylock, Antonio is **representative** of all Christian men who have wronged him. By cutting a 'pound of flesh' from Antonio, he is getting his revenge on Christianity.

Although Shylock's **intentions** are extreme, Shakespeare invites the audience to sympathise with Shylock. We learn that Jessica has not only stolen money from him, but she has also 'stick'st a dagger' in Shylock by stealing an invaluable 'turquoise' ring, given to him by his late wife.

Examiner's Comment

Again, the student is hinting at Shakespeare's intention to condemn anti-Jewish racism here. However, she is not explicit about it. Furthermore, Shakespeare could be sharing these anti-Jewish feelings when he presents the ring as a cause of Shylock's desire for revenge. One interpretation of the ring could simply be that it is both a symbol and a cause of wealth, and so Shylock is just as furious at losing money as he is at losing his daughter.

By being specific about why Shakespeare presents Shylock this way, the student could easily get into the top band.

Additionally, Shylock gives a speech whereby he puts forward some very valid arguments. The **premise** of Shylock's argument is that ultimately we are all human; we are all made of the same substance: 'if you prick us, do we not bleed?'. Yet Shylock has experienced ridicule from **society** and for what 'reason? I am a Jew'. Shakespeare uses a short sentence to **emphasise the injustice** of how Shylock is being treated. This **sentence structure** forces the actor to pause, and so gives the audience time **to reflect** on discrimination **in their own society.**

Examiner's Comment

This is a very specific analysis, with no general points. She is convincing that Shakespeare is trying to control our thoughts. She also uses some evidence about how the lines should be performed, so that she is linking the form of the play to her interpretation. This part of the essay is in the top band.

Shylock's final actions and statements to **portray** his hatred towards the Christian characters are **displayed** in the court room. He is merciless towards Antonio, as he seeks his 'revenge'. **Interestingly**, the Duke's heartfelt appeal for Antonio's life ends by addressing Shylock as 'Jew' as opposed to his name. Referring to Shylock as 'Jew', is somewhat **dehumanising** and once more, **belittles** Shylock's faith.

Unsurprisingly, Shylock responds with 'let...the Jew' have 'his will'. Shylock uses **an element of sarcasm**, referring to himself as a Jew. Here, he is suggesting that if they still can't treat him as a person in his time of need, he can't be expected to 'soften' his 'Jewish heart'. This **is mirrored** in Shylock's earlier words: 'Since I am a dog, beware my fangs'. In this statement, Shakespeare is **conveying** that discrimination causes hate. Shylock's cold 'heart' was caused by hateful actions towards him.

Although Shylock is portrayed as a villain, **the audience are invited to sympathise with** him, especially in the modern day. **Shakespeare addresses issues** of discrimination that are equally applicable now.

Examiner's Comment

The student is now more specific that Shakespeare has constructed the plot in order to challenge anti-Jewish sentiment in his society. She has not fully done this throughout the essay, so that it is not yet conceptualised. She has not fully dealt with the ending of the play, and how this will affect his audience's acceptance of this need for society to be more tolerant.

On balance, this would be Level 5, a "thoughtful, developed consideration", rather than Level 6, a "convincing, critical analysis and exploration". This would therefore be in the mark range of 23, 24, 25 out of 30.

The 19th Century

Charles Dickens (1812 – 1870)

Charles Dickens was a campaigning writer, who wanted to change his society.

Yes, he earned his living as a writer, and obviously he specialised in giving his readers what they wanted. He relished being an entertainer, and sold out tours of England, Scotland, Ireland and America, giving dramatic readings from his books.

But he was also much more ambitious than that. His childhood caused him to become a campaigner for the rights of the poor, and of children who were often put to work at a very young age.

A Christmas Carol and *Great Expectations* both deal with the threat of poverty, the responsibilities of the rich towards the poor, and the thin membrane of luck which often separates those with wealth from those who have lost it.

Charles Dickens was born in 1812, and till the age of 9 grew up on the coast of Kent, just like Pip in *Great Expectations*. Like hundreds of thousands of others, his family then moved to London.

Dickens' father, John, amassed large debts which he couldn't repay. In the early 1800s this meant that he was sent to debtor's prison when Dickens was 12. John's family, his wife and 7 children, were forced to live in prison with him.

Charles was sent out to earn money to keep them, working as a child labourer in a tanning warehouse. Here he was constantly exposed to dangerous chemicals, tar, and the terrible smells for which the tanning process was famous. Although this lasted only 3 months, he saw first-hand what child labour did to his fellow labourers, and he saw how quickly a family's fortunes can change.

We can see how Dickens' yearning for a better life is reflected by Pip and his dream of being a gentleman. Similarly, we can see why he is so keen for Scrooge to help the Cratchitt family, who are close to being destitute.

He worked his way up, beginning working life as a law clerk, then became a court reporter. During this time he wrote his first novel, which was published when he was 25.

He wrote *A Christmas Carol* in 1843 to draw readers' attention to the terrible hardships of the urban poor. More than that, he wanted them to feel responsible. For this reason, he begins the novel with a dying woman starving on Scrooge's steps, surrounded by the ghosts of businessmen. Dickens suggests really clearly how the poor are kept poor by the rich who exploit them.

A Christmas Carol

Charles Dickens wrote this novel quickly.

It was published for Christmas, on the 19th of December 1843, and was written to earn money. Dickens had spent too much money on his tour of America in 1842. He wrote it in the tradition of the Christian Morality Play. For centuries these plays taught the Bible's lessons to the majority of the population, because they could not read or write.

In Dickens' time reading had arguably become the number one leisure activity. So he updated the traditions of the Morality Play. He took the idea of characters representing Christian virtues and sins, and adapted it. He wanted to create characters who had social virtues and sins.

So, Scrooge represents all that is wrong with Victorian society:

1. The rich and middle class believing that the poor deserve to be poor, because they are lazy and immoral.
2. The middle classes believing that prison and the workhouse are enough help to discourage the poor from being lazy and immoral, and encourage them to get paid work.
3. Their belief that consequently those with money don't have any responsibility to those without money. Therefore the wealthy can simply spend their money on themselves and their family, and not worry about the inequality of the huge number of poor people in society.
4. The Cratchitts represent the hard working poor, and Tiny Tim represents the disabled and disadvantaged.

The three spirit guides or ghosts represent:

The Ghost of Christmas Past: memory, innocence, youth, optimism, the idea of cause and effect

The Ghost of Christmas Present: charity, empathy and the Christmas spirit

The Ghost of Christmas Yet to Come: the consequences of our actions, moral growth, the chance to change the future, legacy after death. It also suggests divine punishment and the notion of *memento mori*. This expression means "remember you will die", and used in Medieval times to remind people to give up sinful pleasures like greed and vanity, in order to prepare for heaven.

Dickens doesn't push a heavy Christian message. Instead he uses social institutions like family and Christmas to focus on the human aspect of society. Christmas is so important because it changes how people behave. The problem with simply being Christian and going to church means that everyone can feel they are a good person so long as they pray, go to church and avoid breaking any of the commandments. The rich Christian can get richer, and the poor Christian can pray for help that doesn't come.

So Dickens uses the traditions of Christmas, the family get together, and above all the idea of giving, as a way to suggests that this is how we should all behave as often as possible, not just at Christmas.

The "Ghost Story for Christmas".

Ghost Story for Christmas was the subtitle of the novel. The ghost story is probably one of the earliest genres of story told by our ancestors. It goes hand in hand with the belief in a soul, an afterlife and gods, which predate any existing religion.

Dickens is also writing a ghost story, to be told around the fire. The fire is a safe haven at which to gather and frighten young children with tales of the supernatural.

Christians refer to beliefs and religions which predate Christianity as pagan. Interestingly, by focusing on the ghost story, Dickens is tapping in to our pagan past. Christmas itself was a pagan festival celebrated on the longest night of the year, the Winter Solstice, on the 21st of December. Prince Albert, in 1841, introduced the German tradition of a Christmas tree to Britain. This of course is a pagan symbol.

The original illustrations which Dickens commissioned and paid for showed the ghosts as ancient, pagan figures. Why did Dickens go out of his way to make his story remind his readers of a time before Christianity?

Perhaps it was to suggest that Christian belief is not enough, we have to become better people.

Perhaps it was to suggest that being human has always meant looking after our fellow man, rather than exploiting them.

Perhaps it indicates his own dissatisfaction with the hypocrisy of Christian belief, where a 'good' Christian can do nothing to help the poor.

Perhaps he saw Christianity as only a story: it is much harder to ignore the hardships of the poor if you believe there is no heaven, no afterlife, and only this life, here and now.

Childhood

We might argue that Tiny Tim is at the centre of this book. Without Tiny Tim, would Scrooge have been persuaded to change?

Dickens sees childhood as hugely important. His own poverty as child, you have seen, had a huge influence on him. Children are also a great force of hope. Children do change the future, and Dicken's own life story proves that better than most.

We can definitely argue that Scrooge changes once he sees the world through a child's eyes. Dickens himself made sure that his children enjoyed wonderful Christmases.

Christmas celebrates the birth of a child. Dickens may also have had in mind Jesus's words in the Gospel of Matthew, "Except ye … become as little children, ye shall not enter into the kingdom of heaven". Only by seeing the world from a child's eyes, with their view of fair, and unfair, can we create a fair society. We might call this a heaven on earth.

So many of Dickens' novels: ***Oliver Twist, Nicholas Nickleby, Great Expectations, Hard Times*** focus on children. We can infer that two reasons for this are his desire to create a fairer society, and his desire to create a better future.

Why did childhood matter so much to Dickens?

Well, let's take a look at how society treated children in his day. The industrial revolution had forced families into cities, and large families forced their children into labour.

Children working long hours in fields were tired, but well fed, exercised and fit. In cities, they lived in terrible conditions, with dangerous sanitation, pollution, coal smoke, smog and dust, and worked indoors, starved of sunlight.

In 1844, just after ***A Christmas Carol*** was published, the 1844 Factories Act decided to make children's lives much better. Children aged 9 to 13 were now protected. They could **only** be made to work 6 days a week, instead of 7.

And they **only** had to work 9 hours a day.

Now you can see why Dickens felt society had to change.

The Structure of A Christmas Carol

A Christmas Carol is organised into five "staves", the five lines on which musical notes are written in order to show their pitch. This suggests that Dickens wanted his story to be uplifting and light, like a carol.

We might look at his publication date at Christmas to be a smart marketing move, and a bit cynical – exploiting his readers for money while at the same time asking them to give money to the poor.

But not so fast young reader! Dickens insisted on really high quality printing, binding and illustrations. He demanded 'Brown-salmon fine-ribbed cloth, blocked in blind and gold on front; in gold on the spine ... all edges gilt.' And then he kept the price down, so there was not much profit per book. Why?

Dickens Puts His Money Where his Mouth Is

An obvious conclusion is that it was just as important for him to sell books in order to change society. So, he made them look like very desirable items – they would have looked and felt lovely to a reading public. And then, relative to the book's quality as an object, never mind the story itself, the book would have been seen as really good value.

You have to admire that! I certainly do, and it is why I write my guides in much more detail than my competitors, yet set a low price. Ok, I'm not saving the poor. But I am trying to give you a much higher GCSE grade and, I hope for many of you, a real enjoyment of literature which isn't just about exams.

He also wanted the cost to mean something. The book sold for five shillings. This is why he decides that Bob Cratchitt is only paid fifteen shillings a week. Dickens wants the reader to be able to handle this easy multiplication: 'Bob Cratchitt has to feed and look after his large family, with a full time job, which pays him only enough to buy three copies of this book, the book that you are reading, dear reader, costing five shillings which are little to you, but the difference between life and death to a poor, working family.'

What else is a stave?

Dickens' readers would also be familiar the other meanings of stave. Did Dickens do this deliberately? Well, yes! He doesn't use this structure in any of his other novels. He could just as easily have called the chapters 'verses' if he wanted us to make the direct link with singing a carol.

But he didn't. Let's imagine why.

1. A stave is a post or support in a building – in other words it is used to build something. What does Dickens want his readers to build? That's right, a better future, a better society.
2. To 'stave in' is a verb, meaning to break, break in or destroy. What might Dickens want to break? His readers' perception of the poor? His readers' attitude to social responsibility? The fate of young children like Tiny Tim, or like himself when his father was in imprisoned? You decide.
3. To 'stave off' is a verb, meaning to ward off, or prevent. Did Dickens want to prevent poverty, ward off premature death and suffering, prevent the worst effects of being disabled?

    You know he did.

How to Revise for a Dickens Exam

1. Pick your main character, and relate them to all the main themes of the novel, or what I call the big ideas. For Scrooge it might be social responsibility and welfare, Christian and pagan belief, the spirit of Christmas, social mobility, the power of love, the importance of memory.
2. Then find all the most important quotations about the character.
3. Next, write it all as one giant essay.

Below is my example about Pip, in *Great Expectations*.

(If you are not studying this great novel, look at how I use context, or the 6 Big Ideas about Pip, to make sure my revision is awesome.

If you are studying this text, look out for my guide on **Great Expectations**, because it is going to be beyond Awesome).

Although I have written a lot about social class, every student studying this novel will also do this. So, I am going for a different interpretation, based around patterns of attachment and abuse. Examiners will be much more likely to reward this with higher grades.

Great Expectations

The examiners might just ask you to write about one character. However, they are most likely to ask you about Pip, and his relationship with another character. If you revise this essay, you will be well prepared for any essay that comes up (50% of it anyway!)

The 6 Big Ideas about Pip

1. This is a Bildungsroman, in which we see Pip grow from childish innocence, to social snobbery, and eventual triumph of goodness and love or foolish delusion of love – depending on your interpretation of the ending.
2. Pip is a construct, through whom Dickens explores the effect of social class and the **patriarchy. Dickens links this to how our lives are fated and determined by our social class, no matter how moral, intelligent or hard working we are as individuals.**

3. **Pip is on orphan, with surrogate parents, through which Dickens explores the effect of attachment and parenting adult behaviour and choices. Dickens asks us to consider how far we are heroes of our own narratives, or how far our actions are determined by our repetition of childhood attachments.**
4. **Pip's secret desires are often unexpressed, but acted out by his alter ego, Orlick.**
5. **Pip is a narrator who is not always clear about his motives, through which Dickens asks us to read his tale as a confession, intended to be read by the people in his autobiography.** Only next is it a novel by Dickens, intended to entertain and challenge his Victorian readership.
6. **Pip can only learn to be his true self once he has left Britain, through which Dickens attacks the smothering effects of social class in Britain.**

The bold indicates ideas which are unlikely to be explored in other guides, and which will be a delightful surprise to your examiner should you be writing an essay on Pip!

Great Expectations

This Will Fit Any Essay Title on Pip

- If you are studying *Great Expectations*, grades 7, 8 and 9 are probably on their way from this one essay.
- Sadly, the odds are you are not, but are probably studying *The Strange Case of Doctor Jekyll and Mr Hyde.*
- Whatever you are studying, look at all the words in bold, and try to use them to write about your novel. It will help you get much higher grades.

The Essay

Dickens **constructs** Pip as a thirty-four-year-old **narrato**r of his autobiography, apparently written when Pip is fifty four. The **Bildungsroman** is an entertaining but **socially challenging portrayal of social class** and love. Dickens' **particular emphasis** on (insert whatever the key word of the question is) is designed to (refer back to entertain and the idea of challenging ideas about **society, class** and love).

Pip looks back on his life with a good deal of detached humour in this first chapter. At once, it alerts us to his maturity now, looking back at the errors of his life. But it is also a form of avoidance, of not facing some of the tragedies of his life, and asking us to question the effect of these on Pip. So Magwitch's first words, '"Hold your noise!" cried a terrible voice' alert us to the fact that Pip's childhood is miserable. He is crying. His first action, on learning to read, has been to visit his family's graves, so that he can read their names. **This is a device to gain our sympathies**, but also to ask us **to be critical of the impact** of the various surrogate parents in the novel.

Magwitch will become his benefactor and the father figure to whom he is most devoted. He stays with Magwitch every day while he is in prison, slowly dying from his injuries, even though Magwitch's first words are abusive, threatening Pip with "your heart and your liver shall be tore out, roasted, and ate." He does this even though he later recoils in "horror" from Magwitch because he is a lifelong criminal and possibly murders Compeyson.

This is a **remarkable contrast** to Joe, who Pip continually runs away from. Pip himself feels incredible guilt about this, and cannot understand why he behaves this way to the "noble", "good" and "faithful" Joe. We, **however**, can see below the surface, to his patterns of attachment.

Pip most fears abandonment. He has been abandoned by his five brothers, all dead. By both parents, both dead. His sister and surrogate mother, is Mrs Joe, who beats him regularly with a cane, and literally throws him across the room as a "missile" and squeezes his head against the wall. She has therefore withdrawn any love for him, and continued the pattern of abandonment. We might forgive this, as she has also been abandoned. Pip's humour glosses over any anger at her. But notice he never calls her by name. This is partly an act of revenge. When we consider Orlick as his alter ego, carrying out his secret desires, we see that his attack on her fulfils Pip's wish. It isn't to kill her, but to make her kind.

Now, we can **contrast** this to Joe, who names the cane which she uses to beat Pip as "the Tickler". This is a terrible euphemism. Yes, it is quite funny. But when it is used regularly to beat Pip from infancy to his current age, seven, we can see how cruel the name actually is. Joe's words are gentle, but these hide the full horror of what "the Tickler" does to Pip. Joe is therefore an accomplice, allowing his wife to beat Pip. This provides another reason Pip never uses her name: she is always Mrs Joe because she is a moral extension of Joe. By not preventing her violent abuse of Pip, Joe permits and perpetuates it.

Joe's loyalty to Pip is therefore **ambiguous.** He loves him, and later nurses him back to health, and pays off his debts. But he doesn't invite Pip to his sister's funeral, nor to his own wedding. Pip treats these as his own fault, blaming himself for abandoning Joe. However, we can see he is simply repeating the abandonment he felt from Joe as a child. Pip's adult rejection of this is revealed in his later rejection of being a "blacksmith", his moving to Egypt, far removed from Joe, and his determination to pay Joe back. Although these are all signs of Pip's eventual maturity, they are also hints that he can't fully accept Joe's love, because he does not fully believe in it.

Pip also looks for love from women, but as we have seen, his mother and sister both abandoned him, and Mrs Joe was also abusive towards him. It should be no surprise to us that Pip simply repeats this abusive abandonment in his pattern of attachment towards women. He shows surprising love to Miss Havisham, who is a horrifying figure, when he first meets her, refusing to describe her to Mrs Joe, Joe and Pumblechook, because he knows they will not "understand" her. He is drawn to her precisely because she too has been abandoned by the people she loves – her mother died, her father remarried, he married someone from a lower social class who gave him a son, her father dies, and only finally is she abandoned by Compeyson, the great love of her life.

But, he is also drawn to her because she will repeat this pattern of abandonment with him, and couple it with abuse. She encourages his love of Estella, only to abuse it, letting him know she wants Estella to "break his heart". Yet Pip's attachment to her is so deep that it is almost **supernatural**. He has a vision of her "hanging" from a beam in her brewery on the first day of meeting her. This same vision of suicide returns to him on his last meeting with her, and he rushes upstairs just in time to prevent her actual suicide by "fire".

Although this **supernaturally charged gothic device is a literary type** Dickens knows will attract more readers to his weekly publication of chapters, it is also **to illustrate** the tremendous power of attachment. **He asks us as readers to examine** our own lives because, just as Pip can't see his own patterns of attachment, neither can we. They therefore affect our choice of relationship in ways which are invisible to us. They therefore have an **apparently supernatural effect**, because if we can't see them, we are trapped by them, doomed to repeat the same poor choices again and again.

Estella is also condemned to repeat this pattern of attachment, by turn abusing Pip's love and abandoning him in her marriage to Drummle. Any marriage would have been an abandonment, but the most perfect kind, and the most precise abuse, would be to marry the one person Pip most detests. She does this with Drummle. Pip loves her "against all reason…against all hope". **Dickens wants us to realise** that he is a victim of his pattern of attachment: Pip can't break these habits, even when he realises they are damaging, and Dickens asks us to discover why.

Pip comes to realise the damage caused by his patterns of attachment through his love for Biddy. Even as a young man, he notices that she is "rather an extraordinary girl" who is intellectually "better" then he is and whose beauty is not superficial, but in her "eyes". As a young man, he is not drawn to her because she acts as Estella's **alter ego**, being "common" and neither "beautiful" nor "cruel". His reaction is simply to reproduce his own abandonment – he abandons those he loves.

Once Magwitch has **transformed him**, Pip moves from "horror" to "love". He appreciates Magwitch's love, loyalty and generosity. He recognises that Biddy will bring out these **qualities** in him also, that she will "improve" him, and he travels back to Kent to propose. Here, he is spectacularly abandoned, in that Biddy has literally married Joe that day. Ironically, he is drawn to her at the very moment she abandons him most, both through marriage, and in choice of husband, Joe. Filled with despair, Pip realises he cannot reach maturity and act with genuine free will until he has left Britain, and decides to leave "within the hour".

The novel ends with Pip spending eleven years in Egypt becoming his true self, escaping these attachments. His true love is arguably for Herbert, who is his most constant companion. Herbert **symbolically** gives him new life, saving him from Orlick just at the moment Orlick was going to kill him.

Then Pip is **symbolically** baptised into this new life in the Thames, when he, Herbert and Magwitch are capsized, and Magwitch is caught. In his new life in Egypt there are many hints that he loves Herbert's wife: he even dreams "that I had to give my hand in marriage to Herbert's Clara". Herbert **emphasises** how "happy" Clara will make him.

It is left to the reader to imagine what being **freed from the social restraints** of Britain will produce in their relationship, but Dickens is very clear that it is long lasting and that through Herbert, Pip breaks his pattern of attachment. This also explains why he includes the strange fight with Herbert as "the pale young gentleman". It is the first sign that violence can have "rules", and can be dispassionate, not governed by raging desires such as those of Mrs Joe, Orlick, Molly and Magwitch.

This is Pip's first break with his patterns of attachment, and Herbert **becomes the focus** of all Pip's opportunities to mature. **We see this most clearly** in the lesson he learns from Magwitch, providing Herbert with a useful working life by becoming his secret benefactor. He also **redeems** Miss Havisham, allowing her to rediscover her own moral goodness in continuing as Herbert's secret benefactor.

Finally, we must decide whether he has reached full maturity in his love for Estella. When he meets her as a thirty four year old, he still loves her. She has "softened" and been "bent" into a "better shape".

In other words, Dickens hints that she too has broken her patterns of attachment to men she must hurt. She now has a "heart" and may be prepared to love Pip. Whether or not this ends in marriage, Pip is certain that it will end in their both breaking their patterns of attachment. Consequently, his last words are, "I saw no shadow of another parting from her."

We know that Dickens originally planned an ending in which she refuses him, and remarries, repeating the pattern of abandonment. Now Dickens leaves us to decide whether Pip has ultimately deceived himself. Pip tantalisingly refuses to tell us what happens between the age of thirty four, when this ends, and the time, twenty years later, when he chooses to publish.

In asking us to consider Pip's hidden future, Pip, and Dickens, are also **challenging us to examine our own lives**. Are we able to break our own patterns of attachment and become the heroes of our own narrative?

1797 words.

Did you notice the words in bold are all "subject terminology" you can steal for writing about any text?

What Next?

Now, go through your essay and take it down to a length you can actually write under exam conditions. Here's mine. Unless you are studying **Great Expectations**, it is probably not an essay you need to read! But the idea of making the essay short enough for you to write in 45 minutes is compulsory!

Any Essay Title on Pip (Reduced by 700 words)

Dickens constructs Pip as a thirty-four-year-old narrator of his autobiography. His Bildungsroman is a challenging portrayal of social class and love. Dickens' particular emphasis on (insert whatever the key word of the question is) is designed to (refer back to entertain and the idea of challenging ideas about society, class and love).

Pip refuses to dwell on his tragic upbringing. So Magwitch's first words, '"Hold your noise!"' alert us to the fact that Pip's childhood is miserable. He is crying. His first action, on learning to read, has been to visit his family's graves, so that he can read their names. This gains our sympathies, but also asks us to be critical of the impact of the various surrogate parents in the novel.

Magwitch will become his benefactor and the father figure to whom he is most devoted. He stays with Magwitch every day while he is in prison, slowly dying from his injuries, even though Magwitch's first words are abusive, threatening Pip with "your heart and your liver shall be tore out, roasted, and ate." He does this even though he later recoils in "horror" from Magwitch because he is a lifelong criminal who possibly murders Compeyson.

This is a remarkable contrast to Joe, from whom Pip continually runs away. Pip himself feels incredible guilt about this, and cannot understand why he behaves this way to the "noble" and "faithful" Joe. He imagines it is because Joe is "common," but this is not the real reason Pip is "ashamed" of him. We see below the surface, to how Joe has abandoned him to abuse.

Pip has been abandoned by his five dead brothers and dead parents. His sister and surrogate mother, Mrs Joe, beats him regularly, throws him across the room as a "missile" and squeezes his head against the wall. She has withdrawn any love for him, and continued the pattern of abandonment. Orlick as his alter ego, carries out Pip's secret desires, which isn't to kill her, but to make her kind.

Contrast this to Joe, who names her cane "the Tickler." Joe's words are gentle, but euphemistically hide the horror of Pip's beatings, to which he is an accomplice. Consequently, Pip refers to her as Mrs Joe: she is a moral extension of Joe, who permits and perpetuates the abuse.

Although Joe loves Pip, later nurses him back to health, and pays off his debts, he doesn't invite Pip to his sister's funeral, nor to his own wedding. Pip blames himself for abandoning Joe. However, we can see he is simply repeating the abandonment he felt from Joe as a child. Pip's adult rejection of this is revealed in his later rejection of being a "blacksmith", his moving to Egypt, and his determination to pay Joe back. These hint that he can't fully believe in Joe's love.

Pip repeats these attachments, loving women who will both abuse and abandon him, just as his mother and sister did. Consequently, he shows surprising love to the horrifying Miss Havisham. He is drawn to her precisely because she too has been abandoned by the people she loves – her mother died, her father remarried, then died, and she is finally abandoned by her lover Compeyson.

Pip is also drawn to her abuse, encouraging Estella to "break his heart". Yet Pip's attachment to her is so deep that it is almost supernatural. He has a vision of her suicide, "hanging" on the first day he meets her, and the last, when he rushes upstairs just in time to prevent her actual suicide by "fire". This supernaturally charged gothic device illustrates the tremendous power of attachment. Dickens wants us to recognise we are trapped by our own attachments.

Thus Estella is also condemned to repeat this pattern, by turn abusing Pip's love and abandoning him in her marriage to Drummle. Pip loves Estella "against all reason…against all hope." Pip can't break these habits, even when he realises they are damaging.

Ironically it is Magwitch who transforms him. Pip moves from "horror" to "love" and appreciates Magwitch's loyalty and generosity. When Magwitch dies, Pip recognises that Biddy will bring out these qualities in him also, to "improve" him, and he travels back to

Kent to propose. Yet Biddy has literally married Joe that day. Ironically, he is drawn to her at the very moment she abandons him most. Filled with despair, Pip realises he cannot reach maturity and act with genuine free will until he has left Britain, and decides to leave "within the hour".

The novel ends with Pip spending eleven years in Egypt becoming his true self, escaping these attachments through Herbert, his true love. Herbert symbolically gives him new life, saving him just as Orlick was going to kill him. Then Pip is symbolically baptised into this new life in the Thames, when he, Herbert and Magwitch are capsized, and Pip ceases to have financial expectations. Through Herbert, Pip breaks his pattern of attachment. Consequently, Pip now learns from Magwitch, providing Herbert with a useful working life by becoming his secret benefactor. He also redeems Miss Havisham, allowing her to rediscover her own moral goodness in continuing as Herbert's secret benefactor.

Finally, we must decide whether he has reached full maturity in his love for Estella. When he meets her as a thirty four year old, he still loves her. She has "softened" and been "bent" into a "better shape". She too has broken her patterns of attachment to men she must hurt. She now has a "heart" and may be prepared to love Pip. Whether or not this ends in marriage, Pip is certain that it will end in their both breaking their patterns of attachment. Consequently, his last words are, "I saw no shadow of another parting from her", suggesting an end to the abuse and abandonment. Dickens refuses to tell us if Pip is right, or simply repeating his pattern.

In asking us to consider Pip's hidden future, Pip, and Dickens, are also challenging us to examine our own lives. Are we able to break our own patterns of attachment and become the heroes of our own narrative?

1020 words

(My students who gain grade 9s are able to write 900 – 1200 words, so I hope this length is useful to you).

Charles Dickens: A Christmas Carol

Sample Exam Question

The Ghost of Christmas Yet to Come has taken Scrooge to see a dead body which Scrooge does not realise is his own.

"He lay, in the dark empty house, with not a man, a woman, or a child, to say that he was kind to me in this or that, and for the memory of one kind word I will be kind to him. A cat was tearing at the door, and there was a sound of gnawing rats beneath the hearth-stone. What they wanted in the room of death, and why they were so restless and disturbed, Scrooge did not dare to think.

"Spirit!" he said, "this is a fearful place. In leaving it, I shall not leave its lesson, trust me. Let us go!"

Still the Ghost pointed with an unmoved finger to the head.

"I understand you," Scrooge returned, "and I would do it, if I could. But I have not the power, Spirit. I have not the power."

Again it seemed to look upon him.

"If there is any person in the town, who feels emotion caused by this man's death," said Scrooge quite agonised, "show that person to me, Spirit, I beseech you!"

The Phantom spread its dark robe before him for a moment, like a wing; and withdrawing it, revealed a room by daylight, where a mother and her children were.

She was expecting some one, and with anxious eagerness; for she walked up and down the room; started at every sound; looked out from the window; glanced at the clock; tried, but in vain, to work with her needle; and could hardly bear the voices of the children in their play.

At length the long-expected knock was heard. She hurried to the door, and met her husband; a man whose face was careworn and depressed, though he was young. There was a remarkable expression in it now; a kind of serious delight of which he felt ashamed, and which he struggled to repress.

He sat down to the dinner that had been hoarding for him by the fire; and when she asked him faintly what news (which was not until after a long silence), he appeared embarrassed how to answer.

"Is it good?" she said, "or bad?"—to help him.

"Bad," he answered.

"We are quite ruined?"

"No. There is hope yet, Caroline."

"If he relents," she said, amazed, "there is! Nothing is past hope, if such a miracle has happened."

"He is past relenting," said her husband. "He is dead."

She was a mild and patient creature if her face spoke truth; but she was thankful in her soul to hear it, and she said so, with clasped hands. She prayed forgiveness the next moment, and was sorry; but the first was the emotion of her heart."

Question

> **Starting with this extract, explore how Dickens presents Scrooge's changing beliefs in A Christmas Carol.**

(Remember, the examiners are trying to be kind to you by getting you to start with the extract. They want you to be able to find quotations and start scoring marks. This is why they instruct you: "starting with this extract".

However, the mark scheme doesn't care where you start, or how much you write about the extract compared to the book.

Many students at grades 3 and 4, even 5, struggle to start writing using the extract. If that is you, it is a natural reaction. Instead, start writing about the rest of the novel, and then compare to the extract later.)

Let's revise for this using the published mark scheme.

The **Indicative Content** might say:

AO1

- Scrooge's fear of the phantom, but determination to follow him in order to learn his lesson
- Scrooge's realisation that the phantom is associated with his future and death, and the lesson that he must make the most of his remaining life
- Scrooge began by doubting the existence of Marley's ghost, and the next ghosts, but has now come to accept that they are real.
- He learns that he has been held back by his love of money, whereas he should have held on to love.
- He learns that he does not need to change out of fear of his own death, but fearing the death of Tiny Tim.

AO2

- Language used to describe the ghost and his actions
- Language used by the husband and wife who are glad that he has died, yet ashamed at their unchristian feelings
- Language used to describe Scrooge's feelings
- The build up of Scrooge's learning, from Marley's warnings of torment, to seeing his childhood loneliness, the love of his sister, of his fiancé, the generosity of Fezzywig, to the indifference of everyone to his own death, to the goodwill of others like Cratchit and his nephew.
- How Dickens presents Scrooge at the end of the novel.

AO3

- The Christian message of the novel, and the idea that we will be judged by God and admitted to heaven, or punished in hell.
- The political message, that the welfare of the poor is everyone's responsibility, and the more wealthy we are, the more we should do.
- The literary context – that the ghost story can be used both to entertain and offer a didactic lesson, just like the carols which are sung at Christmas.
- The tradition of dramatic irony where the husband delays telling his wife Scrooge is dead. (You might remember the same device when Macduff is told of his wife's death in **Macbeth**).

So, the perfect way to revise is to use each and every one of these bullet points to write an essay, not under exam conditions.

Can you tell which AO will allow you to write best about different interpretations, and so get the highest marks?

I hope you said AO3!

Now, because I am always trying to get you grade 7 and beyond, my AO3 bullet points are a little more advanced than the exam board will give you or the examiners, especially the last two.

Student Writing: Grade 5 Context

Dickens wants his readers to learn the same lesson Scrooge learns. The wife "prayed for forgiveness" because she is teaching Scrooge a lesson that he should pray for forgiveness too. Better than that, he has a chance to put things right. As Scrooge tells the ghost, "I shall not leave its lesson." We can see Scrooge changing, so Dickens wants us to begin changing too.

Student Writing: Grade 6 and 7 Context

Dickens knows many of his audience are devout Christians. Consequently, he makes the wife who is so glad at Scrooge's death ask for forgiveness, "She prayed forgiveness the next moment".

However, he ends the sentence emphasising "the emotion of her heart", because this will convince Scrooge more to change. Coupling his Christian belief with his emotions is much more persuasive. This is why at the end of the novel "He became as good a friend, as good a master, and as good a man, as the good old city knew, or any other good old city, town, or borough, in the good old world." Dickens focuses on his emotional change, with deliberate reference to his being "good", rather than any reference to forgiveness or God.

Student Writing: Grade 8 and 9 Context

Dickens has also written this ghost story to be read aloud at Christmas. This oral tradition would be partly aimed at children, and delivering a moral lesson. This perhaps explains why the Christian message is given to a child, Tiny Tim, "And so, as Tiny Tim observed, God bless Us, Every One!"

However, it is significant that Dickens paid for his own illustrator, who clearly portrays the ghosts of Christmas as pagan figures. From this perspective, Dickens is promoting beliefs which predate Christianity. Perhaps he is suggesting that the need to be "good" to others is a fundamentally human need. He emphasises this with "the good old world", where "old" tells us that his message is that the need to be good to each other is an ancient and fundamental one.

Perhaps Dickens wants his readers to realise Christian faith is not enough, and instead realise that we need actions now, in the present, to look after the welfare of the poor, rather than relying on a merciful God welcoming the poor dead to heaven.

Student Writing: Beyond Grade 9

Dickens also has in mind a pastoral tradition, where writers celebrated the innocence of the countryside, and a simpler way of life, in contrast to the corruption of London or the cities. This is why Dickens makes the Ghost of Christmas Past take Scrooge to the countryside, where he spent his more innocent childhood: "an open country road, with fields on either hand. The city had entirely vanished."

He emphasises the corruption of London by stating "The darkness and the mist had vanished with it, for it was a clear, cold, winter day, with snow upon the ground." The contrast of white "snow" with the "darkness" of the "city" it has replaced is a warning to his city-bound readers that they too are corrupt, because their cities will have made them so.

This helps the moral lesson Dickens is teaching, that we each carry a bit of Scrooge's self-interest with us, and we could all learn from his example in looking after the welfare of others.

What this means for your Revision of Any Text

1. Revise the context of your text to get the top grades.
2. Link this context to your interpretations.
3. The easiest place to do that is to write about the ending.
4. Aim for grade 9 by writing about the literary tradition and linking it to the author's purpose.
5. Use the indicative content of the mark scheme to write a full answer as part of revision.

Robert Louis Stevenson (1850 – 1894)

Stevenson's best known novels are **Treasure Island** and **The Strange Case of Doctor Jekyll and Mr. Hyde.**

In Long John Silver and Doctor Jekyll he gives us two anti-heroes. They are a fascinating combination of good and evil. Stevenson specialised in characters whose moral compass is different from our own. They are ambiguous. We don't know whether they are more good than evil. He even asks us to question what evil is.

He was born in Edinburgh in 1850. Stevenson was an only child. He had weak lungs from birth, and was often bedridden. From the age of two, he was looked after by a nurse, Alison Cunningham.

From an early age he was interested in the **Bible**. He wrote a prize winning history of Moses when he was 6. At 16, he wrote about a Protestant uprising. His devoutly Christian father paid for it to be published.

By the age of 22 he had given up Christianity. Going to university at 16, he enjoyed the seamy side of Edinburgh, smoking hashish (cannabis) and visiting brothels.

He trained as a lawyer to please his father, but never actually practised. Instead, he trained himself to write by imitating great writers he admired, (which I encourage you to do if you buy the **Mr Salles Guide to Awesome Story Writing**, where I show you how it is done).

He coupled this with a longing to travel. Partly this was medical, to find warmer climates where he could breathe better, and he turned his travels into books.

In 1876, he met Fanny Van de Grift Osbourne at an artists' colony in Paris, with her two children. She was 11 years older than him, but he appears to have fallen in love with her.

She returned to California, and her husband in 1878, but then wrote to Stevenson and he decided to visit her. The journey almost killed him, but he reached California. She divorced her husband and, in 1880, she and Robert were married.

He persuaded her to return to Scotland with him in 1881. There he was inspired by drawing with his 12 year old stepson to draw the map of an Island, and **Treasure Island** was born.

He wrote it as a serial, to be published in a magazine. It is fair to say it revolutionised children's fiction, which had previously been more concerned with teaching children how to behave and make moral choices.

In 1882 he moved the family to the South of France, but had a stroke. He wasn't able to write novels, but found he could write poetry for children. Then came two children's novels, **The Black Arrow** and **Kidnapped** in 1884, when he had now moved to Bournemouth.

Here he had a nightmare. Fanny woke him, and he told her off for disturbing the story of his dream: "I was dreaming a fine bogey tale," he said. He claims to have written the 40,000 word first draft of **The Strange Case of Doctor Jekyll and Mr Hyde** over the next 3 days.

Fanny didn't like it, believing it was too sensational. In her letters she describes burning it. He rewrote it as an allegory in 3 days, then redrafted it for 6 weeks.

Stevenson later claimed it was the worst book he had ever written. But it sold 40,000 copies in the first 6 months, and made him famous.

How Would You use This?

The obvious conclusion is to suggest that Stevenson did not believe in the Christian message of his novel. He introduced it to cater to the demands of his audience. This also invites us to think of his dislike of many of his readers. We can add to that, perhaps, his attitude to the sensationalism in his book. We can read in this a mockery of people like the "maid" and Hyde's "landlady" who delight in the misfortune of others.

We can also infer some sympathy for Jekyll, who is trying to create an alter-ego. Is this perhaps a metaphor for the author himself, creating alternative version of himself in his books? Perhaps too we can see a parallel between his own ill health and Dr Jekyll's.

Interestingly, The Guardian also suggests that Stevenson was using cocaine as a medication against his lung disease at the time. This gives us a drug induced dream as the origin of the story. It also allows us to see the drug taking of Jekyll in a new light. Stevenson might well see it as necessary for promoting life. This suggests that he sees Jekyll's death as a tragedy. It is a death which his readers demand, because it reflects God's justice. He might have hated having to give them what they want!

Life After Britain

Next Stevenson moved to New York in 1887, where they met up with Fanny's mother. Then they toured the South Pacific.

We might read into this a strong desire to escape the corruption of cities and even of western society.

Deciding to live in Samoa is an attempt to enjoy a pastoral innocence. It is free from a Christian idea of sin and moral behaviour. It is free of the need to hide from one's passions and interests. In Samoa, Dr Jekyll would have no need of creating Hyde – we might argue that he would simply be able to be himself, without worrying about society's disapproval of his desires.

Stevenson had a house built in 1890, and remained in Samoa until his death in December 1894, aged only 44.

Jekyll and Hyde Essay

How does Stevenson present Mr Hyde as a frightening character?

Stevenson presents Hyde as a frightening character in several ways. The language used to describe Hyde portrays him as fundamentally 'evil' and 'unhuman'. Stevenson also uses contrast throughout the novella, emphasising Hyde's 'savage' nature. Most prominently, a key motif throughout is the duality of man, represented by Hyde being part of Jekyll. This makes Hyde even more frightening as Stevenson reminds the readers that 'evil' is a part of all of us.

When Utterson first comes face to face with Hyde, he uses sibilance to describe Hyde's laugh as he 'snarled...a savage laugh'. This sibilance implies Hyde's sinister nature. The word 'savage' further emphasises Hyde's threatening persona and portrays Hyde as uncivilised. Throughout this extract, Stevenson refers to Mr Utterson most often, as 'the lawyer'. Lawyers were well respected men and the height of sophistication. By referring to Utterson as "the Lawyer", this creates a sharp contrast with Hyde, who 'gave an impression of deformity'. This further portrays Hyde as an outsider, someone who does not conform to the rules of society, which would have been particularly frightening to Victorian gentlemen at the time.

Furthermore, Utterson suggests Hyde's darkness is more deep-rooted than the 'flush of anger' or the 'savage laugh'. He describes Hyde's face bearing 'Satan's signature'. This reference to the devil implies Hyde's innate evil. However, the signature which is later associated with Hyde is recognised as forged by Dr Jekyll. As Jekyll later explains, the only physical aspect Hyde retains from Jekyll is 'my own hand', his handwriting. Therefore, 'Satan's signature' is that of Dr Jekyll's. Perhaps Stevenson is suggesting that Jekyll too is truly 'evil', as he creates a 'creature' who he is a 'rare luxury', carrying out his 'secret pleasures'.

These 'pleasures' are often uncivilised and sinful. During the rising action in the novella, Hyde performs his most sinful act yet, he murders. The account of the murder is delivered to us by the maid who describes the victim as full of 'old-world kindness' and the murderer as a 'madman...with ape-like fury'. This 'old-world kindness' highlights the innocence of the victim and subsequently emphasises Hyde's frightening character and the monstrosity of his cruel act. The reference to 'ape-like' is consistent with the 'creature' which Hyde is often referred to as. It also suggests that he is not as evolved as his upper-class counterpart, Dr Jekyll. In fact, Victorian upper-class gentlemen often believed that they were more evolved than the rest of society. This reference to Hyde as 'ape-like' supports the common misconception, made by the Upper-class gentlemen, that the lower classes and those who commit crime, are less evolved.

After the murder, Hyde returns to his 'dark and dingy' residence in Soho. Not only does Stevenson uses alliteration to accentuate the darkness of Hyde's house, reflecting his 'dark' character, he also deliberately notes that Hyde resides in Soho. In the 1800s, Soho was associated with poverty and immorality. Thus, for people reading the novella at the time it was published, this association with the immoral Soho, would have portrayed Hyde as even more frightening.

Ultimately, Hyde is most frightening because Stevenson reminds us that evil resides in all of us, just as Hyde resides in Jekyll. Jekyll's biggest revelation, and the one that encourages him to create Hyde, is the belief that 'man is not truly one, but two'. This suggests the duality of man, the belief that man is both good and evil.

In Jekyll's letter, he creates the image of an internal 'war' describing his 'two natures that contended on the field'. The 'field' implies a battlefield in which no man shall prosper. Although both sides of Jekyll technically die simultaneously, Jekyll eventually succumbs to Hyde's will and brings his own 'unhappy life…to an end'.

Hyde would then be free to act 'centred on self', to think about no others and do only what pleases him. Stevenson is suggesting that as we let our 'devil(s)' grow, we lose control of our 'gentle' nature and submit to the temptations of selfish 'pleasures'. This is what makes Hyde particularly frightening, the suggestion that there is a Hyde in all of us, that we too can succumb to our innate immoral drives.

In conclusion, Stevenson presents Hyde as a particularly frightening individual through using contrasting language. Not only is there a contrast between the victim and the murderer (Hyde) but the most obvious contrast is between Hyde and Jekyll. Furthermore, Hyde's actions are unlawful and do not conform to the Upper-class circles he is surrounded by. Perhaps most notably, Hyde is particularly frightening because he represents the evil part of man, which Stevenson suggests dwells in even the most respected of individuals.

Grades 7, 8 and 9

AO1

6. A well structured argument which begins with a thesis.
7. Each paragraph is ordered to build the argument to prove your thesis.
8. Explores at least two interpretations of the character or the author's purpose.
9. You pick really good evidence, or quotations, to back up your argument or interpretations.
10. You write about the full task, which always includes the ending of the text.

AO2

6. Your interpretations of quotations look at individual words and phrases.
7. You sometimes find more than one interpretation of the same quotation.
8. You interpret how the form of the text shapes the way the author wants readers to understand it.
9. You interpret how the structure of the text shapes the way the author wants readers to understand it.
10. You use just the right terminology a student of literature needs to explain ideas.

AO3

4. You write about more than one interpretation. So your thesis argues why one interpretation is better than another.
5. You use details from the author's life, or society, or literature at the time to back up your interpretation.
6. Your conclusion sums up why you have picked one interpretation as more convincing than another. It shows why your thesis is correct.

Student Reflection

I think my understanding and knowledge of how to answer a question to meet exam criteria has developed significantly. Whilst writing this essay, I had in mind the importance of commenting on structure, purpose and context.

Although I think I struggled with commenting on structure, I did succeed in combing context into my answer and noting the author's purpose/effect on the reader. I think I have gotten significantly more confident in writing these answers than I was when writing the 'Lord of the Flies' essay. I am now able to complete an essay in less time also, just as I would be asked to do in the exam.

Additionally, since the beginning of the course I think my use of literary terms has improved; I would have not even considered using terms like 'novella' or 'motif' in an essay before.

You can see from this self-assessment, that I think it is the best way to improve in your essays.

Examiner's Comments: Your Turn

I'm not going to write these for you. Use the mark scheme above to work out how to grade the essay.

Find which bullet points are done less well. If you can mark it, you can write an even better essay, and nail these skills in the exam.

If you are studying the novel, have a go at adding to the essay so that the bullet points are covered.

Essay Based on Extract from The Strange Case of Doctor Jekyll and Mr Hyde

Starting With this Extract, How does Stevenson Present Utterson

Or

Starting With this Extract, How does Stevenson Present Hyde

The Extract

Six o'clock struck on the bells of the church that was so conveniently near to Mr. Utterson's dwelling, and still he was digging at the problem. Hitherto it had touched him on the intellectual side alone; but now his imagination also was engaged, or rather enslaved; and as he lay and tossed in the gross darkness of the night and the curtained room, Mr. Enfield's tale went by before his mind in a scroll of lighted pictures.

He would be aware of the great field of lamps of a nocturnal city; then of the figure of a man walking swiftly; then of a child running from the doctor's; and then these met, and that human Juggernaut trod the child down and passed on regardless of her screams.

Or else he would see a room in a rich house, where his friend lay asleep, dreaming and smiling at his dreams; and then the door of that room would be opened, the curtains of the bed plucked apart, the sleeper recalled, and lo! there would stand by his side a figure to whom power was given, and even at that dead hour, he must rise and do its bidding.

The figure in these two phases haunted the lawyer all night; and if at any time he dozed over, it was but to see it glide more stealthily through sleeping houses, or move the more swiftly and still the more swiftly, even to dizziness, through wider labyrinths of lamplighted city, and at every street-corner crush a child and leave her screaming.

And still the figure had no face by which he might know it; even in his dreams, it had no face, or one that baffled him and melted before his eyes; and thus it was that there sprang up and grew apace in the lawyer's mind a singularly strong, almost an inordinate, curiosity to behold the features of the real Mr. Hyde. If he could but once set eyes on him, he thought the mystery would lighten and perhaps roll altogether away, as was the habit of mysterious things when well examined.

He might see a reason for his friend's strange preference or bondage (call it which you please) and even for the startling clause of the will. At least it would be a face worth seeing: the face of a man who was without bowels of mercy: a face which had but to show itself to raise up, in the mind of the unimpressionable Enfield, a spirit of enduring hatred.

From that time forward, Mr. Utterson began to haunt the door in the by-street of shops. In the morning before office hours, at noon when business was plenty, and time scarce, at night under the face of the fogged city moon, by all lights and at all hours of solitude or concourse, the lawyer was to be found on his chosen post.

"If he be Mr. Hyde," he had thought, "I shall be Mr. Seek."

(Remember, because I know I write at grade 7 and above, I know it is best to start with the extract. If you are not confident in doing this, it is much better to start with the novel as a whole.)

Stevenson questions the Christian setting of the novella by placing the "**church … so conveniently near**." "Conveniently" is ambiguous, perhaps a sign of his devout proximity to God, or perhaps conveying how little effort he wishes to expend in attending church, because it is done only out of convention or duty. The emphasis of "so" suggests the latter interpretation.

Having questioned Utterson's faith, Stevenson presents him as a proxy for the reader, "**his imagination also was engaged, or rather enslaved**" by the "tale". This subtly suggests we have more in common than our "imagination" and being "enslaved" by this great story: we are also suffering from a weakness in our Christian faith.

The description is now filled with suppressed sexual desire, as Utterson **"tossed in the gross darkness"**. "Darkness" works as a motif in the novella, continually reminding us of Hyde's evil, which always symbolises the evil of these hypocritical gentlemen. Utterson appears trapped in this "darkness" which represents his ignorance of Hyde's identity, his fear of Hyde's lack of "mercy", but also that Utterson shares his evil nature. This is powerfully emphasised by the sibilance, suggesting a sinister tone.

The "darkness" is also described metaphorically as "gross", meaning huge and thick. This allusion to impenetrability is emphasised by the "**curtained room**" which represents the theme of concealment which also runs as a motif in the novella, and is dramatized through Jekyll's alter ego's name, "Hyde".

Next Stevenson points to the reason that Hyde is evil: he personifies the evil hypocrisy of Victorian society. Consequently, Utterson fantasises about "**the great field of lamps of a nocturnal city**". This metaphor reveals that London's true nature is "nocturnal", and he emphasises this link to nature calling it a "field".

This prepares the ground for a discussion of Jekyll's true nature, and also that of the other bachelor, Utterson. Contemporary readers would also have noticed that Enfield and Dr Lanyon, the other protagonists, are also bachelors. Stevnson is hinting at what Oscar Wilde called only a decade later, "the love which dare not speak its name", homosexuality.

Consequently, Utterson imagines Jekyll in bed, "**dreaming and smiling at his dreams**" which he immediately implies are dreams of Hyde. He is the figure who Utterson now imagines entering the bedroom and the "**curtains of the bed plucked apart**" is a metaphor for uncovering what has been concealed: homosexual desire. The use of "plucked" is also far more suggestive than 'pulled', as it implies nakedness, just as a bird is "plucked" of its feathers to reveal naked flesh. What is revealed is desire itself, personified by "**a figure to whom power was given, and even at that dead hour, he must rise and do its bidding**." Although this figure, in Utterson's mind, is the mysterious "Hyde", Jekyll is enslaved by the desire for the man "to whom power was given." This is the same "enslavement" of the "imagination" which has affected Utterson's dreams. Stevenson therefore suggests that Utterson shares the same sexual desire.

It is odd that Hyde has already been named, but that Utterson does not name him as the "figure". Stevenson wants us to focus on that oddness, because it means the figure could be Utterson himself, fantasising about a sexual relationship with his great friend, Jekyll.

To allude to this more strongly, Utterson distorts the memory of Hyde as a "Juggernaut" who he now imagines moving at ever increasing speed in a parody of sexual climax, to "glide" and then "**move the more swiftly and still the more swiftly, even to dizziness**". There was nothing dizzy in Hyde's trampling of the girl, this effect is being produced on

Utterson, as a result of his own desires. Stevenson reveals them only in dreams, because they are forbidden. A man who is homosexual is literally lost to society, and Stevenson illustrates this with the metaphor of the city being made up of **"wider labyrinths"**.

Stevenson next employs repetition to suggest that this figure, standing beside Jekyll's bed is not just Hyde, or even just Utterson, but a personification of homosexual desire. Consequently, **"the figure had no face … it had no face, or one that baffled him and melted before his eyes"**. One reason that Utterson can't hold on to the face is that he dare not admit that it is his own. Another reason perhaps is jealousy or sexual curiosity. He wonders what face has drawn Jekyll so successfully that Hyde can now **"blackmail"** him.

The final reference to his face is cleverly ironic. Utterson feels **"curiosity to behold the features of the real Mr. Hyde"**. The emphasis of "real" tells the reader that Hyde is not who he seems. This again is a theme of the novella, because the "real" face of Hyde is of course Dr Jekyll. Hyde is not separate from Jekyll, he is only the evil part of his nature made flesh. But another irony is that perhaps Hyde's evil is just a social construct. He may only be disgusting to a Victorian audience because he is homosexual.

Stevenson makes this as explicit as he dare when Utterson wonders about Jekyll's **"reason for his friend's strange preference or bondage (call it which you please)"**. "Strange" is a deliberate echo of the title, suggesting that Jekyll's duality of man is not just the science which allows him to create a new being, but the revelation this duality is potentially present in all men. "Bondage" is not used here as a modern sexual reference. However, it still implied "enslavement" to desire, and therefore once more suggests Jekyll's sexual desire for Hyde.

Their society dictates that homosexual desire is evil, and for this reason Utterson reminds himself that Hyde's face encouraged Enfield to have **"a spirit of enduring hatred."** We remember that in chapter one, Enfield had to hold back a desire to murder Hyde. Here Stevenson suggests that the social evil is not homosexual desire, but the hypocritical need to suppress it, which leads finally to Hyde, **"the self-destroyer"**, taking his own life, and why his readers demand an ending in which Jekyll is also killed for bringing his desires to life in the shape of Hyde.

Full marks.

My Checklist of How to Write a Literature Essay

As I wrote earlier, you might find this a more helpful way to think about the mark scheme. The mark scheme outlines the skills you must use. This takes the mark scheme and says, "Ok, but what do I actually have to do?"

Go back over the essay, and see how it has done each of these 12 things. Then you will be able to do them in your own writing.

1. Begin an introduction linking the words of the question to the writer's purpose.
2. Keep exploring the writer's wider purpose – what does his novel suggest about their society?
3. Always refer to society, as this will always involve the writer's purpose.
4. Use tentative language to show you are exploring interpretations – e.g. "perhaps".
5. Use connectives which tell the examiner (and remind you!) that you are dealing with alternative interpretations: although, however.
6. Embed your quotations within the sentence.
7. Use words such as suggests, implies, emphasise, reveals, conveys etc, instead of 'shows'.
8. Use literary language that students of literature at university would also use.
9. All novels deal in contrast and juxtaposition, or pointing out similarities – use these words.
10. Always quote from the ending and interpret the ending – this is where the author makes their purpose most clear.
11. Write a conclusion which deals with how the author wants us to view or change society.
12. Try to include a quotation in your last sentence.

Paper 2

How to Use the Essays You Will Find Here

You could just read the essay on the text you are studying. Don't forget to take notes.

But you will learn much more by reading each essay, and the examiner comments that go with them.

You should also try to find the subject terminology, and practise using this yourself.

And of course, you can memorise sections of any essay on a text you are studying.

The Grade Criteria for the Modern Texts paper is the same as Shakespeare and the 19th Century Novel.

1. It will be a well structured argument.
2. It is therefore conceptualised, as you prove the argument through the whole essay
3. It uses a range of judicious references.
4. It will have an analysis of language which is insightful
5. and analyse both form and structure
6. Using judicious subject terminology.
7. It will explore more than one interpretation, including context

The checklist you last looked at on Jekyll and Hyde will also work for the modern texts question.

The most popular text on this paper is **An Inspector Calls.** It is difficult to shine if so many students are answering the same question. How will your answer stand out? The same way it will have interpretations which other students haven't considered. Eventually, I will have a guide for every text you study.

The Mr Salles Guide to An Inspector Calls in available on Amazon. It is more comprehensive, with more grade 7, 8 and 9 ideas than any other guide on the market.

Here's a taster – how you can write about context to get top grades:

J B Priestley, Biography and Context

(The bold sections show you how to use this context when writing about the play)

Priestley was born in Bradford in Yorkshire 1894.

When he writes about Brumley, he is fictionalising a town and people he knows well.

His father was a school teacher.

We can see this reflected in the didactic tone of the play, and how The Inspector works, trying to teach the Birlings a lesson. Priestley is also trying to teach his audience the same lesson.

He wanted to become a writer, but decided not to go to university, thinking he would learn more about the world by experience.

We can perhaps see this reflected in his portrayal of Eric, who went to Oxford or Cambridge, and appears to have learned nothing until The Inspector arrives to teach him about social responsibility.

So, he became a junior clerk at a wool firm when he was 16, in 1910.

This is a similarity with Eva, who also works in textiles. She has probably, like Priestley, begun work there in 1910, because she is tipped for promotion in 1911.

His first piece of writing was published on 14th of December 1912, when he was 18.

1912 is a key turning point in Priestley's life, and is therefore a possible reason he fixes on this year as the key turning point in Eva's life.

It is also when Eva herself becomes a writer, writing in the diary which The Inspector uncovers. It is easy to forget this!

He joined the army in 1914, aged 20, not as an officer.

This choice shows how he would see himself as different to the sons of the wealthy, like Eric and Gerald, who would have joined up or been conscripted as officers.

He was seriously injured in June 1916, came home to convalesce and then trained as an officer. He returned in 1917, but was then gassed, and returned home to work in administrative jobs in the army.

When The Inspector warns the Birlings about learning their lesson in 'fire and blood and anguish', he is talking from bitter experience of the slaughter in the war.

It is probably the war which convinced him to be a socialist.

He wrote autobiographically in <u>Margin Released</u> (1962) of the stupidity of its upper-class generals:

"The British command specialised in throwing men away for nothing … killed most of my friends as surely as if those cavalry generals had come out of the chateaux with polo mallets and beaten their brains out. Call this class prejudice if you like, so long as you remember … that I went into that war without any such prejudice, free of any class feeling. No doubt I came out of it with a chip on my shoulder; a big, heavy chip, probably some friend's thigh-bone."

The officer class would have been made up of men like Gerald and Eric and Birling. The way they treat Eva, as a simple casualty of capitalism is exactly the way he accuses the generals of throwing away the lives of their men, the "John Smiths".

During the war, he wrote poetry and published an anthology privately. However, when he returned he destroyed most copies.

Many students assume that writers just write stuff down. In fact, they agonise over every word. As you see here, there was so much to correct in the poems, that he simply destroyed them. Remember this when we analyse particular words and phrases – yes, Priestley really did mean to use exactly those words, and it really is worth asking exactly why he chose them.

After the war, he went to Cambridge. He completed his degree in two years instead of three.

Arguably this is where he would have met men exactly like Eric and Gerald for the first time. Being older, and having survived the war, he is clearly in a real hurry to make progress in life. We can perhaps see this reflected when The Inspector says "we haven't much time" and in the way Priestley makes Sheila repeat this.

He married his childhood sweetheart from Bradford, where he lived.

Went to London to work as a writer.

He wrote as a freelance writer: reviews, fiction, non-fiction, biography, anything to get published. He worked for a publisher as a reader, and also had four novels published, his fourth being most successful, The Good Companions, in 1929. This novel is a largely comic portrait of people – while it features the working classes, it taps in to the mood of escapism in the 1920s.

He collaborated with a playwright to turn this into a play. in 1932, he began writing plays on his own, publishing Dangerous Corner. He published 50 more in his lifetime.

We can argue that the attraction of the plays is the ability to engage directly with the public and use social commentary. His writing became much more politically active during The Depression in the 1930s.

His publisher, Victor Gollancz, asked him to tour the country to see the effects of The Depression in 1933, and the result of this was published as English Journey, a massive success.

Priestley has a special interest in social reform based on what he has seen of the lives of the working classes and the unemployed. He dramatizes this through Eva, and also teaches his audience by explicitly relating her to "the millions of Eva Smiths, and the millions of John Smiths" in the country.

He became a prolific writer with numerous plays and pieces of autobiography. He also went to America frequently and worked as a script writer.

He became a broadcaster in 1939. He had a very successful radio show during World War 2 which was broadcast as 'Postscripts' which came on just after the news. Although often critical of the government, they were designed to be uplifting for morale.

He was seen by many as the voice of the people after his famous broadcast on Dunkirk:

"But now - look - this little steamer, like all her brave and battered sisters, is immortal. She'll go sailing proudly down the years in the epic of Dunkirk. And our great grand-children, when they learn how we began this War by snatching glory out of defeat, and then swept on to victory, may also learn how the little holiday steamers made an excursion to hell and came back glorious."

You can listen to it here (https://www.youtube.com/watch?v=EYNv4ozHJDw)

We can see here that he is keen to celebrate the ordinary man and woman, and how they can put an end to "hell". This is the same message as his play: vote for socialism, not just for a more just society, but to put an end to war.

He continued to write novels and plays during the war.

Priestley made moral choices, choosing to be good, rather than employed, or secure financially. These personal choices, which his audience in 1945 would remember, give him credibility, an imprimatur of morality. (Look it up, it's a really useful word).

In the 1930s, during the Great Depression, Priestley became very concerned about the inequalities in Britain, and the huge rise in unemployment. He even helped set up a new political party, the Common Wealth Party in 1942. It merged with the labour party in 1945. He stood for parliament as an independent MP in 1945, but was not elected. He was never a member of the Labour Party.

We can see from this how the war increased the public appetite for a more equal society. People could see how unequal society was before the war, and they contrasted this with how massive employment was possible during the war. They noticed millions more jobs for women. People started to ask what kind of future was worth dying for. Priestley deliberately wrote a socialist play to answer that question. He thought a society that cared for everyone else in it, where the rich made sure they didn't exploit the poor was worth fighting for. He wrote the play to change society.

He first performed An Inspector Calls in Russia as there were no theatres available in London.

He still wrote campaigning literature after the war, feeling that a lot of the promise of the 1945 election had not come to fruition in the 1950s.

One piece, 'Britain and the Nuclear Bombs' was so critical at the British development of nuclear weapons that it led to a huge response from readers of the New Statesman. This led to the setting up of CND, the campaign for nuclear disarmament, and Priestley became its vice president.

He was active in the early movement toward a United Nations because he thought it was so important to prevent further wars. He was a delegate to Unesco, where he met his third wife.

We can see in this that he lived out the moral lessons of The Inspector, wanted a society based on people looking after each other, and believing that the greatest threat was future war. When we deal with the ending of the play you will see how it is an attack on war, just as much as an attack on the Birlings' exploitation of the working classes.

He turned down a knighthood and a peerage, as both would be awarded by political parties. However, he did accept the Order of Merit in 1977, as this is a gift made entirely by the Queen, without political overtones.

This allows us to see how critical he would like us to be about the titles in the play: Lord Croft, Gerald's father is so much of a snob he doesn't even celebrate Gerald's engagement to Sheila, who comes from a family he sees as socially inferior. Birling's craving for a "knighthood", not having served his community in any way, reveals why we should dislike him.

He died in 1984 having published over 150 books.

An Inspector Calls

An Essay on Social Class

Written by viewer **Ipthi Chowdhury** – thank you Ipthi!

This essay scores **30/30**

Priestley explores the concept of social class as well as its implementation as a regrettable feature of the early 1900s. Edwardian commitment to social class forms a key aspect of society, which Priestley attempts to challenge. The importance of social class is presented through its impact.

- *Level 3 AO3 Because it is general and not related to the meaning of the play yet. This means it is only showing 'some understanding'.*
- *It also shows you how the examiner is trying to make up their mind as early as possible in your answer.*

In An Inspector Calls, social class is presented as a capitalist and exploitative system. Priestley conveys this reality through Mrs Birling, who attacks Eva Smith's character in a prejudicial manner.

- *Level 4 AO1 – the examiner now feels this is a clear explanation and reference, but it isn't linked to a quotation yet, so isn't really offering a "thoughtful" or "developed" interpretation.*

She describes her as being from "girls of that class". Immediately, Priestley evokes the audience's anger through the use of the pronoun "that": linguistically, revealing the connotations of derogatory feelings on the basis of social status.

- *Level 5 AO1 – Notice how he goes up a level as soon as he links his interpretation to a quotation. It shows "apt references integrated into interpretation", because it is an integrated quotation, embedded in the sentence. Notice that naming "that" as a pronoun earns Ipthi nothing for subject terminology, in AO2 – you don't have to name the parts of speech. In fact, doing so sounds a bit clumsy.*

This would be condemned by the contemporary audience, given the recent war effort in 1945, where the nation united regardless of background, in order to defend Britain.

- *Level 5 AO3 – notice that Ipthi relates this bit of context to the meaning, an attack on capitalism, and to the 'contemporary' audience. Context on its own, as we saw in the introduction, scores low marks.*

Priestley highlights the exploitative element through Gerald's admission, "I didn't feel about her as she felt about me". The theme of upper-class selfishness is recalled here evidently, since Gerald's keeping of Eva Smith as a "mistress" implies he used her, and sexually exploited her, having played with her feelings.

Moreover, Priestley maintains Gerald's **character** as constant, giving his later comments that "everything is fine now". The **irony depicts** the upper-class as callous and uncouth, further **inviting the audience** to **dissociate** from **the social system**.

- *Level 5 A02. So the first reward for terminology is graded "examination of writer's methods with subject terminology used effectively to support". I've placed the 'terminology' in bold. 'Terminology' means the vocabulary you would need to use when writing about ANY literary text.*

Priestley expresses the emphasis on social class as a capitalistic trait, that isn't socially cooperative. This is notable when Mr Birling discusses his business ethics: "it's my duty to keep labour costs down. Our labour costs". Here, Priestley presents Mr Birling as a direct antithesis to social reformation. The possessive pronouns "my" and "our" carry connotations of selfishness and greed, elements Priestley considers to be inherently representative of the nature of capitalism.

Contextually, Priestley evokes the audience's dissatisfaction towards Mr Birling's words. Atlee's newly elected Labour government made increasing social welfare a manifesto commitment in 1945. Mr Birling's business interests would be deemed as counter-productive, following an ideology of extreme austerity. In this way Priestley establishes social class firmly as part of the capitalist economic agenda in the play.

- *Level 6 A01 – the examiner is impressed with this detailed analysis of the use of single words in the quotation. Here it is worth calling them by their parts of speech, because Priestley is using them to emphasise possession, and doing it more than once.*
- *Level 6 A03 – here Ipthi directly relates the context to the meaning of play and Priestley's purpose is persuading his audience to vote Labour.*
- *It's also worth asking if you could memorise the two paragraphs above, and use them in any essay on the play. I think you can, and you will have a level 6 section to your essay, come what may.*

Attitudes towards **social class** are **presented** by Priestley as evolving and important. Priestley **appears** to credit the rise of socialism for the fall of **class hierarchies**, through the younger generation of **characters**. Eric's **development** from being "half assertive" and "half shy", to challenging his father's business **ethics**: "why shouldn't they ask for higher wages?" marks his renouncement of upper-class traditionalism and his adoption of a more **morally** considerate socialism.

- *Level 6 A02 – again I have highlighted the terminology which you would use to write about ANY literature text. There are other words which are specific to **An Inspector Calls**, like 'socialism' etc.*

The question appears as an open challenge to his father and highlights his maturity. However, through Eric **as a construct**, Priestley presents capitalism to his audience as having an illogical and unfair fallacy. Eric's question would have been deemed as reasonable and raise ethical concerns.

- *Level 6 AO2 – I've highlighted 'construct' because it the one word every examiner is drawn to – it is the one which shows you are aware everything in the text is there for a reason, linked to the author's attempt to influence how we think. ALWAYS use it.*

Likewise, Sheila is employed as a construct to challenge upper-class exploitation with a moral argument that, "these girls aren't cheap labour – they're people". The adjective "cheap" further highlights the deplorable upper-class perspective of the lower classes. Priestley's construction of Eric and Sheila as corrigible* attempts to educate the audience that social class is outdated and isn't fit for modern times.

By drawing upon the moral failure of the social class system, Priestley generates odium for it.

*capable of being corrected

- *Again, could you memorise the last two paragraphs and use them to end any essay on the play? I think you could. That's 4 level 6 paragraphs, which will propel your essay leaping over grade boundaries.*
- *All Level 6.*

An Inspector Calls- 100% Grade 9 response on Eric

Written by viewer Ackim Nkole – thank you Ackim!

In his **didactic** play, Priestley uses his play as ***propaganda*** for socialism and is an **allegory** for the hypocrisy of the ***bourgeoisie***. Through Eric, he **constructs** him as a character that was an **outcast** but arguably the most influential character in the play.

In Act 1, Eric was "not quite at ease, half-shy, half assertive". Here, "shy" has implications of nervousness and apprehension, **juxtaposing** the trait of being "assertive" which **connotes** dominance and superiority. This **asyndetic list** creates a sense of him being overbearing and socially awkward. An **interpretation** of this is perhaps Eric is complying to the ***bourgeoisie*** lifestyle and mindset that has been prevalent in his upbringing. Priestley **constructs** Eric in this way to deliberately create a sharp and confusing **portrayal** of him, perhaps making the **contemporary audience** have a negative view upon him. -Level 5 AO2 Method+Meaning

Priestley continues the **negative construct** Eric has received in Act 1. Through the use of his name, "Eric" has origins of Viking and Old Norse tradition, which has implications of violence and oppression. This is important later on as we witness how Eric treated Eva Smith. However, a more **symbolic meaning** of his name comes from a children's book which revived the name during the 19th Century. This is backed up by the description of Eric-"as if I were a child". Here, Priestley **subtly portrays** Eric as child-like, perhaps presenting doubt onto the **audience** that Eric will never change because of his mindset is of a child. Thus, Priestley could be **foreshadowing** that Eric cannot be trusted to ***promote socialism*** and be "one body". -Level 6 AO2 Meaning+ AO1 REFS

(I hope you have worked out that **bold** means vocabulary which is **subject terminology.** ***Bold and italics*** means ***vocabulary*** which is very relevant to high grades when writing about **An Inspector Calls.**

Can you do the same with the rest of the essay? If you try, you will get better and better at using this yourself in your own essays.)

In Act 3, Eric uses colloquialisms to describe his encounter with Eva Smith. He brings normality by claiming his actions are "when a chap turns nasty". This presents Eric as a vile and vulgar man which sends the audience into disgust towards the predicament between Eric and Eva Smith. Moreover, the quote presents a semantic field of violence combined with the past participle "threatened". By doing this, Priestley is suggesting that men in this time period were as obnoxious as Eric, emphasised by the use of colloquial English "chap". By doing this, Priestley is presenting the consequences of a paleo-Conservative government and the Conservative Party has created such moral decay that the bourgeois have the entitlement to feel above the law and malinger around social responsibilities towards the proletarians. As a result, Priestley reveals that the plutocracy isn't fit to take care of the proletarians.

Examiner Comments

Level 6 AO2 Methods AO3 Context. Go back over the paragraph and see if you can pick out why.

Despite his actions, Priestley shifts the negative light Eric has received so far by closely analysing his speech. Eric says "oh-my God, that's how hellish it is". On a simple level it reveals that Eric is feeling compunction towards Eva Smith and poignancy towards her. However on a powerful level, the multiple embedded phrases we saw earlier have been cut down, emphasising the change in character Eric has transitioned to. Moreover, the hyphen brings a sense of lost control, almost as if he's speaking uncontrollably which creates a staccato pace in his speech. By doing this, Priestley shows us we can change our mindset and morality no matter our social group. Furthermore, he emphasises the need to look after one another otherwise it will lead to calamity and deleterious actions such as Eric defiling Eva Smith.

Examiner Comments

Level 6 AO2 Methods and Meaning. Go back over the paragraph and see if you can pick out why.

However, Priestley goes back to the negative mindset as Eric reveals he stole money from his father. This moment is important in the play because Priestley wants to critique the ever-growing hypocrisy of the bourgeoisie. By Eva Smith gracefully declining the stolen money, it presents the proletarian as innocent and pure. Thus complying to the anti-Capitalist message the Bolshevik audience would have. This also presents us that the bourgeoisie are as criminal if not worse than the proletariat which are stereotyped to commit repugnant and abhorrence in this time period.

Examiner Comments

Level 6 AO2 Methods and Meaning. Go back over the paragraph and see if you can pick out why.

Shifting back to a sense of sympathy for Eric, we witness that he is "nearly at breaking point". Priestley has deliberately commanded Eric in this way as a dramatic technique to utilise Eric's acrimony to such peak intensity that he could collapse at any given moment. Furthermore, the word "nearly" suggests that the only thing that keeps Eric conscious in reality is his distain over Mrs Birling. On one hand, we can interpret this as an act of self-actualisation as Eric has realised social responsibility. Alternatively, a Marxist could view this as Eric malingering responsibilities again and despite the shift in character, he will always possess the trait of stubbornness, primarily due to the corruption of the ideology of capitalism. Going back to the former interpretation, Eric says "oh-my God" which reinforces the idea that he has achieved self-actualisation and social responsibility through the allusion of Christian language. Which perhaps presents a need of repentance from Eric.

Examiner Comments

Level 6 AO1 Interpretations. Go back over the paragraph and see if you can pick out why.

In conclusion, Eric is presented as the "famous younger generation" who need to be reformed, educated and instructed on how to create a utopian society(socialism). Through the character of Eric, Priestley constructs him to exonerate the patriarchal and capitalist beliefs held at the time in 1912 and shows we have a choice of picking collective responsibility and abnegating capitalism otherwise it will end in "fire, blood and anguish".

Examiner Comments

Level 6 AO1 Interpretation. Go back over the paragraph and see if you can pick out why.

30/30

The Curious Incident of the Dog in the Night Time

How does Haddon present the ways in which Christopher deals with loss?

(What can I say, the novel is better than the play! The skills and knowledge in this essay are directly transferable to the play. The skills are also relevant to any text you are writing about.)

Haddon presents the ways in which Christopher deals with loss as mainly systematic and logical. Christopher uses reasoning and logic for everything in his life and he deals with loss in the same way, by approaching his situation as a 'puzzle' and forming a 'solution'. Additionally, Siobhan provides him with several coping strategies, combating chaos as Christopher perceives it, to restoring order and logic. He uses these same coping strategies to help him deal with loss.

In the beginning of the novel, Christopher reveals his mother passed away from a heart attack. One way that Christopher copes with the loss of his mother, is by believing that life and death are 'mathematical'. Although he acknowledges that sometimes 'there was a heron who comes and tries to eat all the frogs' he suggests that sometimes frogs and people 'can die for no reason whatsoever', it is 'just…the way numbers work'. The word 'just' suggests that death is impersonal, is 'just' numbers: people die, and people are born and that is 'just' life. Perhaps he is dismissing other people's "needless" emotions which stop them from seeing 'clearly'; emotions cloud logic and facts. Alternatively, the emphasis on the word 'just' could also be suggesting the futility of life. Therefore, Haddon suggests that Christopher's view of death as impersonal and inevitable helps him to cope with the loss of his mother.

Additionally, when Mrs Alexander accidentally informs him that his mother had an affair with Mr Shears, Christopher deals with this loss of innocence by staying focused on the present and voiding all emotion. He informs Mrs Alexander that he will not feel 'sad' because feeling 'sad' about someone who is 'dead…isn't real and doesn't exist…would be stupid'. The use of 'doesn't exist' and 'isn't real' suggests that Christopher does not dwell on the past. Since this happened in the past and they aren't 'around anymore', nothing can be done to change the situation, so it is pointless to be 'sad' about things that you cannot change. Therefore, a particularly useful technique that Christopher deploys to cope with a loss of innocence, is focusing on aspects of his life that he has control over in the present.

Christopher's innocence is most prominently challenged when he discovers the letters in his father's wardrobe from his 'dead' mother. When Christopher discovers that his mother is still alive, he is required to cope with much more than a loss of innocence, but also a loss of order and everything he thought he knew about his family.

Whereas previously he has been able to rely on his logical brain to restore order, when processing this new, shocking information, he emotionally and physically shuts down. He describes the scene as 'like watching a film…but I could hardly feel his hand at all'. The use of this simile emphasises Christopher's emotional detachment from the situation. Perhaps this is his way with coping with a loss of order.

Alternatively, the phrase 'hardly feel' suggests that he is not coping with this new information or a loss of order at all, instead becoming numb. In this way, Haddon displays Christopher's inability to cope with loss.

To regain Christopher's trust after the letter incident, his father reveals that he was the one who murdered Wellington. Christopher processes this information using logic. He surmises that since 'Father…murdered Wellington…he could murder me too'. However, in this case, logic without emotions leads to unrealistic conclusions. Christopher is Ed's son, whom Ed loves wholeheartedly: Wellington was a dog who received more attention from Ed's lover than Ed received from her. Therefore, it is not reasonable to assume that Ed would 'murder' Christopher, just as he murdered Wellington. Thus, Haddon suggests that logic is an ineffective coping strategy and detrimental to Christopher's well-being.

To distract himself from this 'frightening' revelation and the loss of trust in his father, Christopher turns to maths and science. He explains Orion and talks about 'nuclear explosions billions of miles away'. Focusing on 'explosions' could reflect Christopher's current emotional state: all known 'truth' has exploded from his personal life and he is left lost, wondering about a world 'miles away' from where he is now. An escape from his reality perhaps.

Maths and science often offer an escape for Christopher and this is a motif throughout his book. Interestingly, after an emotionally intense chapter, Christopher often devotes the next chapter, solely to maths problems or scientific facts. This structure of chapters reflects the way he copes with loss. When faced with challenging or emotional stimuli, he uses order and logic to calm himself down and help him think 'clearly'.

Notably, Christopher only refers to emotional pain as physical pain. When faced with not being able to complete his A levels, Christopher describes 'the pain in my chest', recognising his pain as physical. The fact that the 'pain' is in the 'chest' suggests that he is experiencing 'pain' in his heart (emotionally). This focus on physical pain can also be seen after he reads his mother's letters; he is 'sick' when his emotional pain manifests physically. To combat this 'pain', he turns to self-harm, hurting himself in various ways, 'so I couldn't feel any other sort of pain'. The use of the word 'other' is the first time in the book where he acknowledges the emotional impact of his losses as a complex emotion. He does not use 'sad' because he recognises that his emotions are more complex than 'sad', too complex to verbalise. Perhaps Haddon is suggesting that self-harm is often a response to not being able to cope with unpleasant emotions.

In conclusion, Christopher often uses logic, science and maths to help him cope with loss. Although these are often an effective coping strategy, getting to London on the train for example, it can sometimes be ineffective and detrimental to his wellbeing (the belief that his father could murder him too). Additionally, due to his emotional detachment, he struggles to process overwhelming emotions, turning to self-harm as a coping strategy.

Examiner's Commentary

This is a candidate who clearly understands the novel, and has a great insight into Haddon's intentions. The paragraph in bold also indicates where she has analysed the purpose of Haddon's chosen form – a novel – and how the chapter structure helps us understand the character.

We can see that she does not just treat Christopher as just a character within the novel. Instead she sees him as construct, whom Haddon uses to explore ideas about how we all process emotion.

The use of the word 'alternatively' signals that she is exploring alternative interpretations. Similarly, using tentative language, like 'perhaps' also indicates interpretations are being explored.

She zooms in on the implications of individual word choice, to make a thorough analysis and exploration of meaning.

However, to be fully conceptualised, an essay really needs to deal with the ending of the novel. This is where the author makes clear their final view. The essay doesn't consider the wider implications of the text, and what it represents about society, relationships or education.

Consequently, this essay would be graded in the top band, but not achieve full marks.

Lord of the Flies Essay

Do you think Piggy is an important character in *Lord of the Flies*?

Piggy is a crucial character in **Lord of the Flies** as he embodies many political, social and cultural issues which Golding addresses throughout the book. Piggy is the only female voice, often quoting his 'auntie'. He is also the embodiment of the working class, as he is the only boy on the island who speaks with an accent.

Examiner's Comment

A strong range of viewpoints, but lacks at thesis telling us what he wants us to learn from Piggy – what will he want us to understand about how women and the working classes are treated? What political, or social, or cultural points is he making? Always be as specific as possible.

Piggy is the only adult and female voice on the island. He often speaks through his 'auntie' and provides adult reasoning, e.g. suggesting that the 'conch' could be used to 'call the others' on the island. Additionally Piggy, unlike Ralph, displays caring characteristics. When speaking to Ralph he mentions 'the kids still in' the plane as the 'storm dragged it out to sea'. The reference to 'the kids' shows that Piggy is empathetic with the boys who didn't make it onto the island. Piggy's caring nature is emphasised by Ralph's contrasting character: when Piggy mentions the lost 'kids', Ralph quickly becomes uninterested in the conversation. Furthermore, Piggy's caring nature is reflected in his task to 'take names', portraying Piggy as a mother like figure, looking after the 'littluns'.

Examiner's Comment

Analysing contrast, here the deliberate contrast between Piggy and Ralph, is a guaranteed way of analysing structure.

Moreover, Golding deliberately makes a link between Piggy and the pigs on the island. This link is made not only in name, but in the pronouns used to describe the pigs: all the pigs are female. Golding uses the boys' mistreatment of Piggy and the pigs to symbolise man's innate violence, in particular violence towards women.

Examiner's Comment

This is an example of being specific rather than general, and sets out the student's thesis well. This is now an analysis of different interpretations.

Sibilance is used to emphasise Jack's sinister nature as he stalks the pig, 'silent as the shadows. He stole away'. The use of the word 'stole' suggests that Jack is about to take something that doesn't belong to him and foreshadows the brutal killing of the pig. He is about to steal the 'maternal bliss' of a mother pig, who is nurturing the 'piglets that slept'. Like Piggy is looking after the 'littluns' on the island, the mother pig is blissfully raising her young.

During the hunt of the pig, the boys treat it as a thrilling game, 'excited by the long chase' they follow her 'dropped blood...right and assured'. The use of the word 'assured' suggests that Jack is confident that he will be able to make the kill. It also implies that Jack believes he is entitled to this pig, perhaps reflecting man's entitlement to women. This entitlement is reflected in the language used to describe the killing of the pig, creating the imagery of violent rape as the boys forced a 'spear still deeper...right up her arse'. This violation of the pig's innocence is foreshadowed by the word 'stole', as the savages are taking more than just the pig's life. So, through the treatment of the pigs and Piggy, Golding is damning men for the view of women and their innately violent behaviour.

Examiner's Comment

This is a very developed analysis of the language used to describe the killing, and it is strongly linked to Golding's purpose. Being able to link this symbolism to male attitudes to women is sophisticated in a novel with no female characters.

Piggy is additionally important as he is a representation of the working classes, the only boy who speaks with an accent. As a reader, Golding encourages us to look down upon Piggy by first introducing him as 'very fat' in a 'greasy wind-breaker'. The adjective 'greasy' suggests that Piggy is somewhat unhygienic. Additionally, Piggy appears to take 'pride' in his disability, 'asthma'. The use of the word 'pride' could suggest that Piggy views his 'asthma' as something that makes him special and different to the other boys. Alternatively 'pride' may imply that Piggy has chosen to be a victim as he revels in his disability. Thus, as readers, we are further encouraged to dismiss Piggy as a character, just as the boys do.

Furthermore, Piggy's glasses are described as 'thick', suggesting that although people with glasses are stereotypically clever, Piggy is 'thick'. This perception of Piggy is supported by his language which is grammatically incorrect, as he states 'I can't hardly move'.

However, Golding is quick to challenge our preconceptions of Piggy by stating that all 'intelligence...was traceable to Piggy'. Here Piggy has the most 'intelligence' and the greatest ideas but is quickly dismissed as an outsider. Perhaps Golding is attacking the very idea of democracy in society. Piggy symbolises someone who should be a leader but is dismissed due to his class; he has fantastic ideas, but cannot articulate them in a way that will make the boys in the 'black cloaks' listen.

Examiner Comment

This is a very confident analysis of a second purpose Golding has in creating Piggy. Having two complex interpretations of the character, and linking these to Golding's point of view, is a skill in the top band – perhaps the most important skill.

In conclusion, Piggy is a very important character as Golding uses him to symbolise many motifs throughout the novel. Through Piggy, Golding portrays men's innate violence towards women. He also uses Piggy to suggest that the leaders in society are perhaps not always those with the best ideas. He suggests that we should not dismiss those of a lower class to us because class is not mutually exclusive with intelligence or kindness.

781 words

Examiner Comment

Although demonstrating so many of the skills of the top band, there are elements missing. The discussion of women is developed enough to satisfy AO3 analysis of context. The discussion of democracy is less developed.

In order to be 'conceptualised', the student should probably deal with the reason Piggy is killed – why doesn't Golding allow him to survive, instead preserving Jack and Ralph?

My advice is always to deal with the end of the character and the end of the novel, whatever the question. This is the easiest way to show you have considered the full text. It is also the easiest way to give a convincing argument about the author's final intentions.

As with the previous essay, this has many of the skills of a top band response, but because these are not fully developed, I would grade it as 7.

What Should I do Now?

So far, all our essays have rewarded the same skills. The poetry comparison, coming up, is slightly different.

Let's take a moment to consider how you should revise from the book so far:

1. Pick out the key 'subject terminology', and make a list. Use it to write your own paragraphs or essays on texts you are studying.

2. Pick out the essays on texts you are studying. Make notes, or mind maps on these. Leave it a few days. Then try to write the same essay yourself. First, without your notes (this will improve your memory). Then, with your notes, to improve it. Then compare it to the original, to see what you have missed out.

3. Pick out key quotations from the essays, and link these to themes you have studied. Then link these to characters.

4. Write about the ending of each of your texts, and link these to the author's purpose.

5. Write about the context of your text, and link these to the author's purpose. Do separate paragraphs for the social context of the time, the author's life, and the literary context (which most students ignore!)

6. Use my 12 point checklist to writing a top grade essay to rewrite an essay you have already written. Get your teacher to regrade it for you, and see how you have improved.

7. Look at the 5 big ideas about patriarchy, Christianity, social hierarchy and class, education, fate and free will. Write your own paragraphs about each one of these in relation to the texts you are studying.

8. Practise writing the opening thesis for each of the main characters. Remember that you want to link each character to the big ideas or themes – this will propel you to the top grades.

9. Find alternative interpretations for the ending of each text. Memorise quotations from the ending. Write practice paragraphs where you explain this.

10. Use the past paper mark schemes, and the indicative content, to write your own essay. It will be too long! Practise writing the same essay, in fewer words.

Poetry Anthology

Romanticism

Romanticism was a reaction against the Enlightenment which dominated the 1700's. A very broad summary is that the Romantics did not look for absolute truth, either in science or religion. Instead they saw truth or genius in ordinary things, especially nature.

In the Enlightenment, rich Europeans used to travel around Europe, visiting the great cities, studying Greek and Roman art and great architecture.

The Romantics did this, but were just as likely to search out experiences, nature and political activism in their travels. They wanted to change the world, rather than just glorify the past. This meant that the individual became much more important than conforming to society's values. Society, they would often believe, desperately needed change.

It is interesting that Romanticism was much more popular in Protestant countries such as Britain, Germany and America, and had much less influence in Catholic countries such as France and Italy.

It was characterised by a belief in freedom, not just religious, but also political freedom, free from the rule of the monarchy or tyrants such as Napoleon. It also meant freedom from class. But, in the lives of Shelley, Byron and Blake in particular, it also meant freedom from society's values, especially around sexuality and moral behaviour. For Shelley and Byron it meant freedom could only be found by leaving that society. For Byron and Wordsworth, it probably led to love of, and incest with their sisters. Different times!

For poets this meant "the spontaneous overflow of powerful feeling," a definition created by Wordsworth. This also meant that poets did not feel that they had to maintain classical forms of poetry with rigid rules and structures. Instead, like Wordsworth, they allowed each poem to find its own form.

Many poets also rejected poetic language which they felt was artificial, and tried to use language which was closer to everyday speech. They were much more comfortable writing about ordinary lives, rather than poetry which focused on heroic figures, epic events. This is typical of Blake and Wordsworth.

Blake and Wordsworth were both powerfully influenced by the French revolution, not just in their politics, but in seeing poetry as a means of changing how people thought about life, politics and art. A modern poet might be thrilled to sell 1000 copies of their anthology. Our 19th Century poets often sold in the tens of thousands, and became household names.

Their ideas mattered, and they wrote believing they could change the world.

William Blake (1757-1827)

William Blake was a Romantic poet who lived through the French and American revolutions. He supported both, unlike most British people. He was strongly critical of the king and government. Although a devout Christian, he was very critical of the church for not using its power to help ordinary men and women. He was a visionary, who saw visions of angels throughout his life.

He was not at all famous as a poet. Most of his poetry didn't sell. Instead he made his living as an engraver and artist. He began writing poetry in his teens. However, by then he was already an apprentice engraver. At 21 he trained briefly as an artist at the Royal Academy of Arts, but he fell out with the senior lecturer, and left.

So, he was a self-taught artist. He published each poem with an accompanying illustration.

His political views were radical, and quite different from most of society.

At 25, he married Catherine Boucher, and taught her to read and write. Then he trained her as an engraver. He was an early campaigner for women's rights.

His most famous poetry collections were **Songs of Innocence** and later **Songs of Experience** but sold hardly any copies.

Recurring themes in his poems are protest against monarchy and war, and against the church and society for allowing social inequality. He celebrates the power of the imagination and the individual.

He was incredibly intelligent, and taught himself Greek, Latin, Hebrew and Italian so that he could read important texts in the language in which they were written.

His art work and poetry were not appreciated by the general public. However, both Coleridge and Wordsworth recognised his poetic talents. So, he was a genius, and hardly anyone knew or cared!

London by Willian Blake

I wander thro' each charter'd street,
Near where the charter'd Thames does flow.
And mark in every face I meet
Marks of weakness, marks of woe.

In every cry of every Man,
In every Infants cry of fear,
In every voice: in every ban,
The mind-forg'd manacles I hear

How the Chimney-sweepers cry
Every blackning Church appalls,
And the hapless Soldiers sigh
Runs in blood down Palace walls

But most thro' midnight streets I hear
How the youthful Harlot's curse
Blasts the new-born Infants tear
And blights with plagues the Marriage hearse

Form
This is written in quatrains, with a simple ABAB rhyme scheme. This helps Blake write it as a didactic poem, because the form echoes the sort of structure found in a poem for children. In this way, he points out that his message, that our rulers are oppressive and corrupt, is easy to understand. The simple form also makes it easy to remember, and for Blake's readers it would have been a matter of routine to memorise poems in order to be able to recite them.

Opening
I wander thro' each charter'd street,
Near where the charter'd Thames does flow.
And mark in every face I meet
Marks of weakness, marks of woe.

Blake contrasts the freedom of nature to the oppression of the city and those in power. So nature, in the form of the "Thames" is allowed to "flow" freely, in contrast to the people in each "charter'd street". This phrase also complains about ownership. Common land has become controlled by the monarchy, the government and the church, and even the river has been sold off. This symbolizes how citizens' freedoms have also been sold off.

However, the other contrast is with the poet's persona. The poet is still able to "wander", which symbolises his freedom of the mind. Poetry has given him liberty, just as he wants his poem to help us see how we can liberate ourselves from oppression.

SOAPAIMS

(This is a mnemonic for any language feature, of which there are dozens. The most crucial are listed in the glossary at the end of this guide. The very short version SOAPAIMS is taught in many schools: Simile, Onomatopoeia, Alliteration, Personification, Adjectives, Imagery, Metaphor, Senses, so I include it here)

"The mind-forg'd manacles" is a powerful metaphor, suggesting slavery or imprisonment. On one level, he suggests that our rulers have been cunning in finding ways to enslave us – they have made the social systems that keep the poor from wealth seem natural.

On another level, he asks us to look at our own minds. Have we created our own "manacles" by accepting a social order that allows us to be ruled by the aristocracy, unlike the French who have recently executed most of the nobles in their revolution?

Similarly, do we blindly follow a belief in God who will reward us in heaven, so that we will simply accept inequality on earth?

SOAPAIMS

How the Chimney-sweepers cry
Every blackning Church appalls,
And the hapless Soldier's sigh
Runs in blood down Palace walls

I can write about any of these lines as my second example. They are all packed with symbolism. However, we are being strict with ourselves.

So, I'll focus on the line "Every blackning Church appalls". This is an attack on the role of the church, which should be defending the interests of the poor – Jesus campaigned for the rights of "the meek", but instead the church allows child labour and early death to be commonplace. The church has such authority, argues Blake, that it could simply take a stand which would stop child chimney sweeps being employed.

There is a bitter secondary meaning to the word "appalls". The primary meaning is that this child exploitation shocks those within the church, but the Bishops simply ignore this and stay silent. Metaphorically, the church is becoming evil, as suggested by "blackning".

But the secondary meaning of "appalls" is to cover the church with a black "pall". This is a cloth of mourning, placed upon a coffin. Here Blake argues that the church is already dead. He is predicting the rise of atheism. Unlike later 19th century writers, he isn't arguing that the advances in science prove the Bible is a work of fiction. Instead, he argues that the organised church has no moral authority, and from this people will conclude that God, however real or illusory, has abandoned us.

You could say just as much about the metaphor of the "Soldier's sigh" or the "Palace walls", but you don't have time!

Structure

The frequent anaphora, emphasising "every", implies that no part of society is free. This implies that even the rich do not really benefit from their financial advantage, they are still victims of the "manacles" which prevent them thinking free thoughts, and experiencing life as it should be.

Ending

This is emphasised by the ending. Here Blake tells us that he has saved his most conclusive point till last, so he starts "But most". This final point is not about the rule of government, monarchy or the church.

Instead it is an attack on males, and their corrupt hypocrisy in their patriarchal relationship with women. Yes, Blake was a feminist, as you remember from his education of his wife and treatment of her as his equal.

Here men turn their marriages into a "hearse". This is metaphorical. They kill their marriages through prostitution, causing the "Harlot's cry". But also, their pursuit of sex means there are so many prostitutes, which is why theirs is the most common "cry".

However, this also literally kills the marriage, through the spread of venereal disease. There were no antibiotics in Blake's day. The treatments, such as taking mercury, were just as lethal as the disease. Wives would contact venereal diseases without knowing, and these would also deform their children, as we see in the "Blasts" which ruin the "newborn infant".

Above all, then, this poem is a strong attack against the patriarchal behaviour of men.

Lord Byron

George Gordon Byron, (1788 – 1824)

Byron was the most famous of the Romantic poets, both for his poems, and his scandalous private life.

Born in 1788, his father died when he was three. He inherited his title of Lord in 1798. He went to Harrow, then Cambridge where he became well known for keeping a bear as a pet, walking it like a dog.

He was widely described as beautiful, despite having a club foot. It is believed he refused to allow lovers to sleep in his bed, so they couldn't see it. He was the kind of person who felt incomplete without a lover, and wrote in a letter, "'I cannot exist without some object of Love' (Lord Byron to Lady Melbourne, 9 November 1812)".

He became famous for his long satirical poems, and then his long Romantic narratives. These were so successful that Sir Walter Scott, one of the country's leading poets, actually abandoned writing poetry, and moved to novel writing. Byron called him, Keats and Wordsworth fools.

He was happy to make enemies, and desperate to be noticed.

He was famous for having numerous affairs and lovers, both male and female. Byron cultivated this in his public persona. His final poem, Don Juan, was an account of a legendary lover. In 1812, he had an affair with Lady Caroline Lamb, who apparently made the affair too public, so he ended it. She described him as "mad, bad and dangerous to know" which is ironic, as she then tried to stab herself.

Her revenge was to write a novel in which the main character is a portrait of Byron. In the modern world we send abuse in 140 characters of Twitter, but in Byron's day they knew how to turn 'beef' into literature.

In 1814, his half-sister Augusta gave birth to a daughter, who was widely believed to be his, as a result of incest.

In 1815 he married Annabella Milbanke, and with her had his only legitimate child. They separated in 1816.

He left England to live in Italy and fight in Greece. He never returned to Britain.

He spent the summer of 1816 at Lake Geneva with Percy Bysshe Shelley, his wife Mary Shelley, Mary's half-sister, Claire Clairmont, and his young doctor, John Polidori. In typical Byron fashion, Claire became his lover, and with her he had a daughter. And it rained a lot, so there wasn't much to do. Byron set them all the challenge of writing a ghost story.

Byron wrote one of the first vampire tales in English, "**A Fragment**". John Polidori also tried to write, as Mary recalled, he "had some terrible idea about a skull-headed lady." Apparently he argued violently with both poets, and left. In 1819 he published **The Vampyre**. Most readers made the connection between its villain, Lord Ruthven, and Byron.

It became an international best seller and inspired Bram Stoker, in 1897, to write **Dracula**. Polidori had actually been paid £500 to keep a secret diary of the trip, by Byron's publisher, so he could record the many scandals the publisher knew Byron would be involved in! Lady Caroline Lamb published her novel in 1816, Glenarvon, and had based the villain on Byron, calling him Lord Ruthven…

What a world.

Shelley was inspired to write two of his most famous poems that summer, **Intellectual Beauty** and **Mont Blanc**. He apparently gave Byron lots of advice on his poem, **Don Juan**. What will you do in your summer holidays?!

Then to Italy, where he had an affair with an Italian noblewoman, Teresa Guiccioli.

He died of a fever in Greece in 1824. At the time his writing reveals he was probably in love with a 15 year old boy, who didn't return his affection.

Byron published **When We Two Parted** in 1816, claiming it was written in 1808. His private letters reveal this was to protect the identity of the lover it describes, Lady Frances Wedderburn Webster. In 1816, she had a public and scandalous affair with the Duke of Wellington, the general who had defeated Napoleon in 1812, and therefore probably the most famous man of his time.

Consequently, his separation from her was caused by Byron's leaving Britain to escape his debts, and to protect his sister Augusta from the scandal of their suspected incest.

His protests at being "deceived" are a little hypocritical, given that he immediately got Claire pregnant. As you will read about in my section on Shelley, he later insisted she hand over their daughter and leave him in Italy.

Naturally, we can't know any of this for certain, and by keeping the identity secret, Byron is trying to speak to readers who have been rejected by their own lovers at some point in life. His very personal story is trying to reach a universal truth.

Even a hypocritical, vain, cruel, mad, sexist cheat like Byron still believed in a better world. That's why he fought for the Greeks in their war of independence. And it is why he believed Art existed with a capital A, to transform our experience into universal truth and beauty.

That's the Romantics for you.

When We Two Parted

When we two parted
  In silence and tears,
Half broken-hearted
  To sever for years,
Pale grew thy cheek and cold,
  Colder thy kiss;
Truly that hour foretold
  Sorrow to this.

The dew of the morning
  Sunk chill on my brow--
It felt like the warning
  Of what I feel now.
Thy vows are all broken,
  And light is thy fame;
I hear thy name spoken,
  And share in its shame.

They name thee before me,
  A knell to mine ear;
A shudder comes o'er me--
  Why wert thou so dear?
They know not I knew thee,
  Who knew thee too well--
Long, long shall I rue thee,
  Too deeply to tell.

In secret we met--

   In silence I grieve,

That thy heart could forget,

   Thy spirit deceive.

If I should meet thee

   After long years,

How should I greet thee?--

   With silence and tears.

Analysis

Form

This poem doesn't share the strictness of rules Shelley, Browning and Blake imposed on their poems. Instead, Byron loosens the reigns of control. So, each stanza is eight lines long, but he allows each line to have 4, 5 or 6 syllables.

We might suggest that this is to reflect the emotional content of the poem, which feels personal. The poem explores his feelings for an ex-lover, and because he has conflicting emotions, he allows himself room to explore them.

He does impose a tight rhyming structure, of ABABCDCD. We might decide he rejects rhyming couplets because the lovers are now parted, apparently acrimoniously, and couplets suggests a couple still intact. Instead, each stanza has two four line patterns, reflecting how the lovers are in counterpoint, rather than harmony: they clash.

Many critics point out that the lines do have a pattern of dactylic dimeter. This means that they have two stressed syllables per line. Some critics argue that it gives the poem an uncomfortable rhythm, full of hesitations, to reflect the speaker's uncertain mood. Well, it gets you marks.

Instead, look for lines when this pattern is broken, as it will reveal an emphasised emotion or point. For example in "half broken-hearted" I'd argue that he breaks the dactylic dimeter. Here the first syllable of each word is stressed. This implies that he is more than "half broken-hearted" and more miserable than he would like to admit, he is wholly broken hearted.

Opening

The opening "we" suggests that the poem is written to the ex-lover. The passive "were…parted" suggest neither lover broke off the affair. Instead we imagine circumstance parted them. To readers, it strongly suggests one or both of them were married, and events with their partners caused the separation of the lovers.

Autobiographically, they parted because Byron went to Geneva to escape the bailiffs. He uses the passive as a way not to write, "ok, we parted because I was irresponsible with money and had to flee the country. I know it was my fault. I'm sorry." In other words, it allows him not to accept responsibility.

The phrase "Half broken-hearted" is ambiguous. It may indicate that neither had fallen fully in love with the other. Their affair was exciting, sexual, but not based on love.

Alternatively, now that the persona looks back, he may feel that he was wrong to feel this way. Time away from her has made him realise that he is broken hearted, while her new affairs suggest that she was not. He now realises he loves her, but she never loved him.

"To sever for years" also implies an agreement that, when circumstances change, they intended to renew their affair "years" later. Now news of her new affair makes him accuse her, "Thy vows are all broken", so he knows the affair will never resume. "All" is perhaps ironic, suggesting that she has also broken her marriage vows, which should be her worst fault. However, to the lover, breaking her "vows" to him are more cruel.

SOAPAIMS

Byron uses metaphor ambiguously, "And light is thy fame; / I hear thy name spoken,/ And share in its shame. /They name thee before me."

"Light" might imply that she is only briefly famous, for an act which has caused "shame". But this might also be used as a contrast to his own "shame" and "fame", so that he would stress the word "thy", suggesting his own is heavy, or dark. Both these meanings would fit autobiographically with his infamous reputation.

There is also a contrast between the inconsequential sounding "light" and the sinful sounding "shame." This suggests that people are more forgiving of her, presumably for her new affair with a prominent man. Whereas, they are less forgiving of him.

A final irony might be the persona's realisation that his emotions also include jealousy. Her name is put "before me", meaning in front of: people are talking to Byron about her public affair with a later lover, not knowing he was once her lover, as this is "secret".

A further possibility is that "before" also means above, or more important. His fame is being eclipsed by hers, perhaps because he is 'mad, bad and dangerous to know', whereas the public are much more forgiving of her public affair.

A further possibility is that "light" suggests her fame is the opposite of substantial, just temporary. Read this way, her actions in having a public affair are simply to become famous, to be involved in a public scandal. Here the persona could be suggesting that her fame will not last. She is, as we might say now, just a wannabe.

This is an interesting possibility. Why would a woman risk being part of a public scandal? She would only do it, in this patriarchal society, if it gave her more power and influence. It may be that, being the lover of a powerful man, she would then have access to the powerful in society. It may also be a from of advertising, proof of how desirable she is, so that her next lover would need to have the same economic or social status if she were to become his mistress or lover.

SOAPAIMS

The poem is packed with alliteration, sibilance and consonance (where consonants are repeated anywhere in the word except the beginning). Harsh 'c's and 'k's suggest how uncomfortable the speaker is. The sibilance emphasises his sense of loss caused by the end of their love affair. We can see this in the first stanza:

"Colder thy kiss; /Truly that hour foretold / Sorrow to this."

Again in the second: "I hear thy name spoken, / And share in its shame."

And repeatedly in the fourth: "In secret we met-- / In silence I grieve", and "With silence and tears."

Because the sibilance ends the poem, and replaces the earlier harsher sound, we realise that sorrow is his overwhelming emotion. Now he has stopped blaming his lover, and feels instead sad at the loss of her love.

We might also infer from the "silence" he claims that this poem wasn't initially intended for publication. He doesn't want readers to identify his lover. It feels like a poem, written in reflection, for himself. Consequently, it feels autobiographical.

Structure

By the way, the examiners would be perfectly happy to consider the italicised paragraphs in the FORM section as proof that you have analysed 'structure'.

An interesting aspect of structure is his asking of two questions, one of which is unanswered: "A shudder comes o'er me--/ Why wert thou so dear?"

We must therefore answer it for ourselves. It may be that he now looks back incredulously, and asks himself how he could ever have loved someone who didn't deserve his love. She has broken "all" her "vows", she likes to "deceive", and he now views her with disgust.

However, it may be that he now wonders how he so completely misunderstood his own feelings. Now he believes they shouldn't have "parted", that he was in love with her, she was "so dear" but he simply didn't realise this at the time. In this reading, he is shocked at himself.

Which version do you prefer?

Ending

"How should I greet thee?--/ With silence and tears."

One reading of this is that he imagines meeting her after many years, and deciding that his only proper response is "silence". Here he would still respect her need for secrecy. Alternatively, it might mean the opposite, that he feels contempt for her – he cannot imagine even speaking to her, and so his "tears" reflect either his anger, or his grief.

Another possibility is that "should" might hold its modern meaning here. In this reading, he implies that he knows he should feel resentment and anger, but won't. This hints at the possibility of forgiveness, and even a desire to rekindle the affair.

You decide which interpretation you prefer!

Percy Bysshe Shelley (1792-1822)

Shelley developed both his poetry and his political views as a child. He was born during the French revolution, in 1792. His father was a landowner, and a member of parliament, so he was always going have strong political views. He was also the eldest of seven children, which we can imagine made him take on responsibility at a young age.

At the age of ten he went to boarding school, and aged twelve went to Eton. Here he was bullied physically and mentally, and we can easily imagine him developing a dislike of the privileged upper classes.

His isolation also spurred him to live in his imagination, and to write. By the age of 18 he had written and published two novels and two books of poetry. This was the year, 1810-1811, in which he went to Oxford.

Shelley also rebelled against society's Christian view, publishing a pamphlet with his friend Thomas Jefferson Hogg, **The Necessity of Atheism**. He and his friend were expelled or 'sent down'.

He didn't just rebel against social norms in his thinking, he also rebelled in his behaviour. He became a vegetarian. He eloped with a girl his parents had forbidden him to see, a 16 year old Harriet Westbrook, marrying her in secret. However, he soon fell in love with a school teacher, Elizabeth Hitchener, dedicating a book of poetry to her.

He also published political pamphlets at this time, inspired by his hero, William Godwin. Harriet gave birth to Elizabeth in 1813, and by 1814, while she was pregnant with his next child, Shelley left her.

He had fallen in love with Mary Godwin, the daughter of his political mentor, William. Her mother was also Mary, Mary Wollstonecraft, the author of an early feminist book, **A Vindication of the Rights of Women**. Shelley and Mary fell in love while courting at her mother's grave, and there are rumours that they consummated their love in the graveyard. Again, we see Shelley breaking society's taboos, this time in a gothic fashion.

Their whole relationship can be seen as an act of rebellion. Godwin was horrified. Shelley and Mary fled to Paris, and her father disowned her for three years. They took Mary's sister Clair with them, and toured Europe for six weeks. Mary was also 16 years old.

They returned within the year, and Mary was pregnant at the same time as Harriet. Harriet gave birth to Charles, sued for divorce. Mary gave birth to a girl who died a few weeks later. They lived with Clair in London, and, because they believed in free love, sources suggest that Shelley encouraged Mary to have an affair with his friend, Hogg, while he had an affair with Clair.

In 1815 Shelley inherited £1000 a year from his grandfather, which made him financially independent for life. She got pregnant again, and give birth in 1816 to a son they called William.

Perhaps reacting to the intensity of her relationship, the death of her first child, and replacing it with another, in 1817 Mary wrote one of the century's most famous novels, Frankenstein, when she was aged only 19. Shelley remained a prolific writer during this time.

This novel was also inspired in 1816, when Mary's sister began an affair with Lord Byron, as you have already read. In fact Clair had set out on this trip specifically in order to have an affair with Byron. Fame is like that. Clair, Byron, Mary and Percy shared a villa in Switzerland, where Shelley began to write about the power of nature.

Mary's step sister Fanny committed suicide in 1816, as did Shelley's wife Harriet, in December. We can easily see how Shelley would be very aware of the effects of time, and the tragic brevity of life. We might infer from this that his writing was not just a spur to create a better world, but also to preserve something of himself for history. That certainly works for me as an interpretation of his intentions in **Ozymandias.**

He married Mary on 30th December 1816, apparently hoping that this would mean he could get custody of Elizabeth and Charles. However, because he was an atheist, the courts refused to allow it!

In 1817 he moved to Marlow, where he got to know the poet Keats and the artist Leigh Hunt. He wrote a book whose main characters committed incest, which his publishers refused to publish, so he rewrote it. This does indicate that there was no taboo too great for him to break.

In January 1818, he wrote **Ozymandias**.

In 1818 he and Mary decided to live in Italy, taking her sister Clair with them, so that she could introduce her daughter to her father, Lord Byron in Venice. The Shelleys moved from city to city. Their son died of a fever in Rome. A year later their daughter Clara also died. Byron demanded that, if he were to look after his daughter, Alba, Clair would have to leave her in his care. Clair left her daughter behind.

Shelley's fourth child, Percy, was born in 1819.

At this time, Mary Shelley wrote a book, **Matilda**, in which the main character commits suicide after her father develops an incestuous love for her. Critics see it as an attack on the patriarchal society, and point to the fact that though she is the victim, Matilda is still punished in the afterlife.

Shelley continued to write poetry and political pieces prolifically, for the rest of his short life. On the 8th July 1822, he drowned while sailing his schooner with two other crew members, who also drowned.

We can see in this biography a desire to experience life to the full, no matter what the consequences. We can also see the great sacrifices they were willing to make for art, and writing. Every part of their lives seems to have been devoted to personal freedom, the breaking of social boundaries, and the desire to promote experience above all else.

Ozymandias, by Percy Bysshe Shelley

I met a traveller from an antique land,

Who said—"Two vast and trunkless legs of stone

Stand in the desert. . . . Near them, on the sand,

Half sunk a shattered visage lies, whose frown,

And wrinkled lip, and sneer of cold command,

Tell that its sculptor well those passions read

Which yet survive, stamped on these lifeless things,

The hand that mocked them, and the heart that fed;

And on the pedestal, these words appear:

My name is Ozymandias, King of Kings;

Look on my Works, ye Mighty, and despair!

Nothing beside remains. Round the decay

Of that colossal Wreck, boundless and bare

The lone and level sands stretch far away."

Form

Shelley has deliberately chosen a sonnet form. Firstly, because it is traditionally a love poem. This is ironic, because it points out Ozymandias's self-love and hubris. The poetic persona would normally express love, but here he expresses scorn, turning Ozymandias's "sneer" back on the ruler.

Secondly, a sonnet is a classic form, handed down to us from Roman poets. This highlights the enduring power of art, which clearly outlasts the power of even the most powerful ruler. This is also reflected in the physical remains of Ozymandias's empire, the broken statue and his carved face. As we shall see, Shelley will celebrate the skill of the "sculptor" above the power of Ozymandias.

A further level of irony here is that Shelley himself acknowledges he hopes the fame of his poem might well outlast the kind of fame Ozymandias has. And it is true. Name me a prime minister from Shelley's life time? You probably can't, but you can name at least two other poets or poems from the same period. Power to the poet!

Opening

"I met a traveller from an antique land,

Who said—"Two vast and trunkless legs of stone

Stand in the desert. . . . Near them, on the sand,"

The poet distances himself from what he is describing, so he only finds out about it from a "traveller". This might be because this is a political poem, attacking all rulers. Ozymandias is therefore not just a historical figure, but represents the British aristocracy who hold on to corrupt power, because it is unelected.

Another reason might be historical. The ironic fact is that Ozymandias's boast, "Look on my Works, ye Mighty, and despair!" is not that hubristic. Do a Google Image search and you will find statues of him all over Egypt and north Africa. Shelley might know that his poem is in fact built on a lie.

Far from being forgotten by history, Rameses II left a huge impression and physical legacy. Giving the story to a traveller allows him to say, "well, this is just what I have been told, don't blame me if the facts are wrong!"

Another way he tries to distance us from this inconvenient truth is by changing his Pharaoh name, Rameses II, to Ozymandias, which is what the Greeks called him.

A further reason for the Greek name is to remind us of the Greeks, the fathers of democracy. It is therefore ironic to give such a powerful enemy of democracy, a dictator, a Greek name. Shelley is therefore pointing out that democracy will overcome dictatorship, that the future will be better than the past.

The reference to "sand", which is echoed at the end of the poem, symbolises the passage of time. Shelley is pointing out that political power is temporary. On the one hand, this is a campaign for democratic elections. On the other hand, it points to his passion for poetry and art: he believes that he will leave something much more valuable behind than those politicians and Lords who spend their energy on controlling others with the same "cold command" as Ozymandias.

SOAPAIMS

"And wrinkled lip, and sneer of cold command,"

The repetition of "and" lists the many undesirable features of Ozymandias's expression, to suggest his many faults as a ruler. The alliteration of "cold command" suggests his cruelty and lack of emotion. It also suggests that his pursuit of power also gave Ozymandias an unfulfilled inner life – he is "cold" in the sense that he is missing a fundamental human need, warmth, and connection with others.

We can see that this has actually damaged him, so that even his "lip" is "wrinkled", as though he has prematurely aged by denying himself personal connections with other people (which makes him very similar to the Duke in **My Last Duchess**).

SOAPAIMS

"The hand that mocked them, and the heart that fed;"

This is a doubly useful line, because it also introduces the Volta, which will allow us to hit the structure mark as well. The Volta is Latin for 'turn', and occurs at line 8 of a sonnet. That is why I have set the sonnet out with this layout, so you can see it.

The metaphors in this line suggest that Ozymandias "mocked" his people, and maintained his power through a symbolic cannibalism, as he "fed" on, we presume, his people.

But at the moment of the Volta, we can also read this as a description of the "sculptor". Here, the sculptor has skilfully mocked Ozymandias by carving such a damning portrayal of him. His art has come from "the heart", and Shelley is pointing to the emotional impact of the sculptor's art.

In this interpretation, the artist does feed on others, but art also feeds others. The sculptor's work is therefore a gift, and consequently his art still has meaning thousands of years later.

Structure

We have already scored all the marks we need, discussing the Volta.

We can add to that the half rhyme of "stone" and "frown" and "appear" and "despair". These are unexpected. Perhaps this echoes the other ways he wants to challenge our expectations, claiming that art is much more important than material success or political power.

Or to surprise us that dictators, such as the contemporary Napoleon, will become irrelevant in years to come. The poem was written in 1819, and the Napoleonic wars had lasted from 1803 to 1815, most of Shelley's life. The poem then becomes a celebration of life, and a call to forget the effects of war, and look to a better future.

He soon decided to move to Italy, both as the home of renaissance art, but also in rejecting the a society in Britain which has been militarised by the war with Napoleon. By 1828, the military commander who had defeated Napoleon became prime minister. In other words, Shelley recognises that British society was shifting towards a more military and authoritarian one. His poem speaks out against it, and he backed this up with his actions, choosing to live in Italy.

Ending

"Round the decay

Of that colossal Wreck, boundless and bare

The lone and level sands stretch far away."

The assonance of "e" and "a" in the final line sound like a lament, perhaps to mimic the sound of despair which Ozymandias himself might feel at what has become of his empire, buried beneath the "sands".

The alliteration of "lone and level" symbolises Ozymandias's own personal loneliness, ruling without love. "Level" further indicates how completely all his monuments and buildings have been obliterated, so they leave no imprint behind. The only thing that survives of him is his face, in the work of the artist, the sculptor.

This is celebrated in the allusion to classical art and the Colossus of Rhodes, one of the seven wonders of the world. This statue is also a "wreck" (having fallen on to the shore after an earthquake). So on one level it symbolises Ozymandias's great vanity and ephemeral fame.

On another level, it symbolises the power of art to transcend time – the Colossus is still famous even though it no longer exists. In this way, Shelley is hoping his own art will last forever. However, this is not just his own vanity, as he celebrates "the sculptor", suggesting that this makes art itself one of the wonders of the world, which will survive for millennia.

Robert Browning (1812-1889)

Let's spend a moment thinking about a world without exams. Where students went to school to learn the greatest ideas in history.

You want to learn history? Ok, then we'll have to teach you Latin.

You want to learn literature, and politics and drama. Ok, we'll have to teach you ancient Greek.

You want to travel? Ok, let's teach you Italian and French because, hey you already know Latin.

You want to take your place in society? Then you need to know how to play music, how to dance, how to look after a horse and ride.

The idea that you would go to school and learn at the same pace as every other student your age was just nonsense. Time is short!

So, Browning sounds to a modern audience like some kind of bizarre genius. Born in 1812, he learned Latin, Greek and French by the time he was fourteen. He was also taught dancing, drawing, horsemanship and music. At 12 he wrote his first poetry anthology. At 13, he read everything ever written by Shelley, and in imitation of him became a vegetarian and an atheist, like his hero. We all have heroes. It's just that in Victorian Britain being a poet was considered very cool indeed, in the way that you might dream of playing electric guitar and fronting a band.

Like Shelley, he started university, but dropped out. He wrote poetry and plays from 1828, but gave up playwrighting for poetry, though he perfected the idea of the dramatic monologue in his poems.

He corresponded with Elizabeth Barret, a much more famous poet, in 1844 – they met, fell in love and married in 1845. Like Shelley's marriage, this was against the wishes of her father. Again like Shelley, they eloped to Italy, to Pisa and Florence.

Although he continued to publish poetry, he was better known as Elizabeth's husband. However, she died in 1861, and Robert and their son returned to London. The poems we study come from **Dramatis Personae**, which he published in 1864. He gradually became famous after this time.

Porphyria's Lover, by Robert Browning, (written in 1836, when Browning was 24)

The rain set early in to-night,
    The sullen wind was soon awake,
It tore the elm-tops down for spite,
    And did its worst to vex the lake:
    I listened with heart fit to break.

When glided in Porphyria; straight
    She shut the cold out and the storm,
And kneeled and made the cheerless grate
    Blaze up, and all the cottage warm;
    Which done, she rose, and from her form

Withdrew the dripping cloak and shawl,
    And laid her soiled gloves by, untied
Her hat and let the damp hair fall,
    And, last, she sat down by my side
    And called me. When no voice replied,

She put my arm about her waist,
    And made her smooth white shoulder bare,
And all her yellow hair displaced,
    And, stooping, made my cheek lie there,
    And spread, o'er all, her yellow hair,

Murmuring how she loved me — she
    Too weak, for all her heart's endeavour,
To set its struggling passion free
    From pride, and vainer ties dissever,
    And give herself to me for ever.

But passion sometimes would prevail,
    Nor could to-night's gay feast restrain
A sudden thought of one so pale
    For love of her, and all in vain:
    So, she was come through wind and rain.

Be sure I looked up at her eyes
    Happy and proud; at last I knew

Porphyria worshipped me; surprise
    Made my heart swell, and still it grew
    While I debated what to do.

That moment she was mine, mine, fair,
    Perfectly pure and good: I found
A thing to do, and all her hair
    In one long yellow string I wound
    Three times her little throat around,

And strangled her. No pain felt she;
    I am quite sure she felt no pain.
As a shut bud that holds a bee,
    I warily oped her lids: again
    Laughed the blue eyes without a stain.

And I untightened next the tress
    About her neck; her cheek once more
Blushed bright beneath my burning kiss:
    I propped her head up as before,
    Only, this time my shoulder bore

Her head, which droops upon it still:
    The smiling rosy little head,
So glad it has its utmost will,
    That all it scorned at once is fled,
    And I, its love, am gained instead!

Porphyria's love: she guessed not how
    Her darling one wish would be heard.
And thus we sit together now,
    And all night long we have not stirred,
    And yet God has not said a word!

This is the shocking story of man who kills his lover because he realises that at this moment she loves him, but that in the future she will leave him. She'll leave because he is her social inferior, and their love is therefore hidden, and won't be accepted by society.

He kills her, he imagines, gently. He uses her long hair, which he wraps sensuously around her neck, three times, each turn a little tighter. It is a kind of foreplay, which is why she allows it to happen, and dies with her eyes shut, as though at peace.

However, his desire isn't sexual. Instead, he sits her dead body next to him, placing her head on his shoulder as he sits alone with his thoughts, until he finally speaks them to us.

His confession is full of passion, humour, anger and deceit. In the final line he appears to challenge God to punish him, either in defiance or welcome. We can't be sure.

Form

Although it tries to mimic natural speech, it is written with a strict rhyming pattern, ABABB. The rhyming couplets are perhaps an echo of his desire to remain a couple. You might describe the asymmetrical pattern as reflecting the irrationality of the speaker.

I have set the poem out above in its logical, rational form, so that each stanza clearly reflects this pattern. But, in your anthology, there are no stanzas. This is Browning's deliberate choice, to unsettle his readers. He has changed the expected form (the one I've given you) to the compressed version. It is a clear signal that his speaker has the wrong form – it hints at his madness, and proves his lack of clear thinking.

It is another dramatic monologue and another dramatic confession. Unlike the Duke of **My Last Duchess**, who feels he can get away with murder, there is the possibility that the last line hints at the speaker's desire for punishment. Alternatively, it is an attack on Christian morality – if there is no God, why should we fear acting on any of our desires?

Opening

The subject matter is typical of Romantic poetry. The stormy weather, the night time setting, the cosy isolated cottage, the image of rural perfection are all present at the beginning, in a tribute (a homage) to the pastoral tradition.

But this is done ironically. The weather echoes that of the storm which brought Frankenstein's monster to life. Just as the subtitle of that novel, **'The Modern Prometheus'** launched Romanticism as an attack on God, so this speaker launches his attack on God.

Although Browning doesn't refer to Frankenstein, we know how much he was influenced by Shelley. We can imagine how he takes the themes of **Frankenstein**, and runs with them in this poem.

In **Frankenstein**, the scientist Victor takes the place of God, usurping him, and creating a monster which leads to his own destruction. The book is partly written as Victor's confession. This poem is an exact parallel. Just as Victor becomes the true monster, the speaker in this poem becomes a monster.

Another similarity is that the tragic events of Frankenstein are arguably triggered by society's rejection of the monster. And it is society's objection to the male lover which leads to his crazed desire to possess Porphyria, as though he can freeze the moment of her adoration forever.

Prometheus is punished by Zeus. He is chained to a mountain side. An eagle rips open his side and eats his liver. Prometheus, being immortal, lives through this, his liver regenerates, and he wakes up the following morning where once more an eagle rips out his liver…

Porphyria's lover tries to stop time as a reward, rather than his punishment, and then appears to dare God to punish him. Although Zeus does punish Prometheus, he is eventually freed by Hercules. There is a sense that Porphyria's lover believes that God will eventually forgive him.

The name Porphyria seems to have been made up by Browning. It derives from the Greek word for purple. There are many possible reasons for this choice:

1. The Greek origin suggests that the poem is pre-Christian, and suggesting that God is therefore not real, and won't punish the murderer.

2. Purple is the colour of royalty, and Browning is suggesting she is murdered because of her social status. Social class is the evil in society which has created this murderer.

3. As a result of being strangled, the colour of her face will be purple. The lover doesn't mention this, as he is so determined to believe his own fiction, that she died loving him and at peace, rather than in extreme agony.

My personal guess is that the second interpretation is the one that educated Victorian's would find most believable, which lends weight to an interpretation that this is mainly an attack on social hierarchy.

We also see the same theme in **My Last Duchess**, Browning's other poem, which I will deal with fully in my guide to the Poetry Anthology.

SOAPAIMS

However, Browning departs dramatically from the Romantic themes of Wordsworth and Blake, by exploring sexuality. This is much more the territory of Shelley and Byron. Her "soiled gloves" are symbolic of the way she has gone against social ideals of purity, by taking a lover.

In the patriarchal society, we have seen two versions of this. In one, the young woman, or girl as we would now say, finds a Shelley, or a Browning, and chooses them as lovers who will later become husbands. In the second version, they seek out men of fame, as Clair does with Byron, as Lady Webster does with the Duke of Wellington.

These affairs are tolerated by society, by which I mean male society, because they place men firmly in control.

But Porphyria is dramatically different. She comes from a higher social status. She keeps her lover's identity secret. He is male, but lacking power in the relationship. So we can see this poem as an allegory for men's desperation to hold on to patriarchal power.

Consequently, shockingly for Victorian times, Porphyria takes the lead sexually, directing her lover's "arm about her waist". Then she partly undresses, and "made her smooth white shoulder bare". When he fails to respond, she places his "cheek" on her shoulder and then more sensually covers him with her blond, "damp" hair. He imagines the sexual pleasures they will enjoy comparing it to "to-night's gay feast", from which she has just come, a metaphor for sexual appetite.

What stops her seeing him as a potential husband appears to be society. "Pride, and vainer ties" suggests her reputation would be damaged. He suspects she will finally reject him, realising his "love of her" is "all in vain".

Structure

As you can see in my rendering of the poem, it is written in stanzas of five lines. However, it is not published that way. This jars the reader, finding it in one single stanza. The structure is deliberately unsettling as the speaker is. Similarly, the rhyme scheme of ABABB is unbalanced, just as Porphyria's lover is in his motives. We might add that the constant return to a rhyming couplet reflects his attempt to hold on to Porphyria's love for him forever, believing that he can do so even in death.

Ending

However, he does not kill her out of jealousy that another, richer man will marry her. Nor does he do it out of anger because she will leave him. Instead, he kills her because, for the first time, he realises she loves him, "at last I knew/ Porphyria worshipped me; surprise/ Made my heart swell." The shock of this discovery makes him react to preserve that love forever, in a way he knows is impossible in real life.

The Romantic poets, as you know, risked everything for love. They spurned society's rules, and lived on their own terms. In this reading, Browning is the lover, refusing to conform. Here, he punishes Porphyria for conforming, for not living and loving as her true self.

So, her lover kills her because she has broken society's patriarchal rules. But Browning kills her because she has not pursued true love, and given in to society's rules in keeping her love secret.

Ironically, however, he punishes her just as society would. Her crime is social transgression, first in having sex outside of marriage, secondly in assuming a position of power over a man. But, finally and most importantly, loving someone socially inferior.

Porphyria's Lover was first published under the title "**Madhouse Cells**". The logic of this suggests that social prejudice has led to the lover's madness. Society prevents people from following their love and passions, and therefore those passions are dangerously transformed. So he tries to preserve her love forever, or at least for one night, focusing on her "smiling" and "blue eyes" which "laughed".

The final couplet "And yet God has not said a word!" can be interpreted in a number of ways.

God has not "said a word!" because God is a social construct, and has no power because He does not exist. If this is the speaker's point, it also suggests that a belief in God will benefit society, because the murder might never have taken place if the lover believed God's power was real. So, to a contemporary reader, the poem might be a warning against atheism.

Alternatively, this is an attack on a very real God, who has stopped seeking to help mankind. We might read into this the Victorian obsession with crime in their society, and the idea that it is growing out of control.

Or it might simply reveal the madness of the speaker to a Christian audience, who believe that eternal damnation in hell is far worse than any punishment he might receive now, if he gets caught. If he is not caught, that freedom is illusory, because eternal punishment is, well, like forever.

Alternatively, it is an attack on the status quo, and the patriarchal society which allows a man to believe he can get away with murder simply because the victim is a woman. Patriarchal power is so deranged that the killer can even imagine that his lover welcomed her death, as we see in his description of her "laughing" eyes.

His madness is therefore not an individual thing. Browning uses the lover to express the views of men, that women are only an extension of themselves and that everything about them, even their lives, are simply men's possessions.

Don't Read This Section Unless You Want Grade 9!

(When you study A level you begin to look at different 'critical theories'. You can use these to look beneath the surface of texts, to ask what is really going on. Often, they will help you see that the author is not always in control of their own choices, and it will give you interesting ways to interpret the characters' choices.

Although I am applying these to **Porphyria's Lover**, some of you will want to apply these to all your texts).

Critical Theories

Feminist Perspective (A way to look at the patriarchal society).

Porphyria is the victim of a patriarchal society. Her lover demands to see her as a possession, and kills her in order to possess her. The ending points out how absurd this patriarchal ambition is. The man who owns her has nothing. She is dead. All he owns is his guilt. This guilt is the one society should have, for killing women in this way.

Porphyria is ironically the named person in the poem, and a social superior to her lover, both forms of status. However, none of this status is enough to overcome the sexism of society. This is why she is punished for her sexual desire. Even more because she is not dependent on a man – she has not had to marry him – and because she initiates sex.

Even his sexual response is an image of bondage and slavery – he ties her up and strangles her with her own hair. In other words, he kills her with the symbols of her femininity. In this way Browning highlights how women are objectified and controlled, so that even their natural sexual desires are forbidden and dangerous.

Marxist Perspective (A way to look at class and social hierarchy)

The Marxist perspective would see her as a symbol of class. Class, and social snobbery, have warped her perspective. This has meant that though she loves him, the class system meant she also "scorned" him.

In this reading the upper class superiority is just a veneer, like the "soiled gloves" and her "white skin".

Social oppression by the ruling classes then leads to the lover's madness.

Although we can't side with him, we understand that society has driven him to madness. Had Porphyria been blind to class, the two would have remained happy, and so she would have remained alive.

In a Marxist interpretation, Christianity is also a means of oppressing the lower classes. Christianity teaches us to accept the status quo, to "render unto Caesar what is Caesar's" as Jesus tells us. Christians can interpret this to mean that justice and reward will come in heaven, after death.

To a Marxist, this simply allows the rich to hang on to power and wealth, and prevents the workers from rising up and overthrowing their oppressors.

The rise of Marxism is therefore directly linked to the decline in Christianity. It is why Karl Marx called religion the "opium of the masses", suggesting that Christianity is both an illusion, and a tool for keeping people drugged, and incapable of thought and action.

A Marxist interpretation will see the end as a reminder of the power of the masses, easily able to overthrow the power of their social betters as long as they realise the decision to rise up is not mad. There is no God to punish them for revolution. In this reading the lover seems mad, but later events will prove he is not. He'll get away with it!

Christian Perspective

A Christian interpretation is more difficult. However, we can see that Porphyria is killed because of her sexual sin – she lusts after someone outside of marriage.

So, in a Christian sense, she will be judged as sinful. True, eternal damnation is not a sentence men can give, and the lover has no authority to murder her.

From the Christian perspective, the lover's challenge to God is not a signal that God does not exist, but simply proof of the lover's madness. Just as we know Porphyria will not be preserved in this frozen tableau by her lover's side, so we know his sense of escaping punishment also won't be preserved. The contemporary reader fully expects him to be caught and punished in this life, and for eternity, like, forever.

Literary Context: Monologues

Browning's monologues made him a unique poet in his day. He entered into the psychology of his characters. Because many of his characters are evil, he challenges his readers to imagine what his own thoughts might be.

The monologues are deliberately provocative, and each poem also works as a kind of short narrative. Every story demands us to ask for a moral, and perhaps that's another reason he chooses to write in the voice of so many immoral characters. It is another way to challenge us.

Another way to distance himself from the people he wrote about was to set them in history, such as **My Last Duchess**, or abroad.

They also force the reader into the role of a detective. What is the speaker leaving out? Who is he talking or confessing to? Why is he confessing? They are psychological portraits and we are asked to understand their psychology.

Psychoanalytical Theory

This theory is created by Sigmund Freud. It claims that the personality consists of three different elements, the id, the ego and the superego.

The Id

The id is driven by basic drives and needs, like hunger, thirst, and libido (sexual desire). The id acts in order to avoid pain and find pleasure. The id acts on impulse and often pays no attention to the consequence of these actions.

The Superego

The superego is moral, concerned with right and wrong. Instead of acting instinctively like the id, the superego wants to act in socially acceptable ways. It judges us, using guilt to encourage socially acceptable behaviour, choosing right over wrong.

The Ego

The ego tries to compromise or balance the id and superego. It tries to find ways to satisfy the Id in ways which are socially, or morally acceptable. The ego will try to defer short term pleasure if it can see a long term benefit for the individual.

Psychoanalytic Interpretation

A psychoanalytical interpretation would look at the dangers of the id having too much control. Porphyria's lover is almost entirely controlled by his id. He is in open rebellion with the superego, which he sees as the control provided by the class system.

He also realises that Porphyria is controlled by that superego. Her ego has satisfied the desires of her id, to take this lover. But he realises this is only temporary, and that she will soon reject him because of his social status.

However, his id is also afraid of hers. His response to her taking the sexual initiative, and making him subservient to her, is punished with death. Perhaps his superego is at work here, punishing her for the ultimate transgression of being a woman in a patriarchal society who has both social and sexual power over a man. This causes a rupture in his personality, which he cannot control. So, to re-establish control, he kills her.

His descriptions of Porphyria are diminutive – he focuses on "her little throat" – as a symbol of his control, which will fit all the interpretations. It can show how, as a male, he cannot see her as superior, nor even as an equal. So he describes her as "little".

A psychoanalytic interpretation will see the ending as evidence that he has been driven mad by his id, believing he can keep Porphyria's love "still" and forever.

Some readers interpret his confession as sexual insecurity. This is why he doesn't respond to her sexual advances.

Consequently, he describes himself in the third person, "one", to distance himself from that insecurity: "one so pale / for love of her, and all in vain." He is "pale", and "in vain" has tried and failed to respond to her sexual confidence. In other words, they argue, he cannot achieve and erection. He is impotent.

The Patriarchal Interpretation

It was first published under the title of 'Porphyria'. At the time, perhaps Browning did not see it as odd that he didn't allow her to speak. She has no voice in the poem. In other words, when he wrote it, Browning may well have shared a patriarchal view, and been quite used to seeing men holding power as simply more natural.

Thirty years later, as he matured, he looks back on this and changes his mind!

Thirty years later, perhaps, Browning has become more convinced of the damaging sexism of his society, and makes it more explicit that male power is the problem, making us focus instead on 'Porphyria's Lover' by changing the title. Now he is pointing out to us that he knows she is treated as unimportant by society. She is not allowed to stand up for herself, and we only get to meet her through the perspective of the male lover.

Now Browning wants us to focus on his male behaviour as an allegory of how all men have an unequal power relationship with women, and to point out that this is destructive.

And obviously you can find autobiographical details from Browning's life (detailed above) to show that he was, for his time, a bit of a feminist.

Feminist Interpretation of the Murder

Well, obviously, we could analyse everything in detail, but just knowing this bit inside out will be plenty.

That moment she was mine, mine, fair,
Perfectly pure and good: I found
A thing to do, and all her hair
In one long yellow string I wound
Three times her little throat around,
And strangled her.

"Moment" reveals his knowledge that her love for him is temporary, and soon she will no longer be his.

The repetition of "mine" reveals his desperation to keep her love, but also to keep her as a possession.

The alliteration of "Perfectly pure" reveals that he wants her virginity, as symbolically both "pure" and perfect. This is also ironic, because she is clearly no longer a virgin. The only way she is "pure" in his mind is in her "worship" of him. He kills her, rather than let that moment of "worship" pass.

He is unable to name the act of killing at the start, it is just "a thing to do". But this casual language also reveals his lack of guilt – it isn't that he can't face calling himself a murderer, it is more that he simply doesn't care – the important thing is that he has possessed her, and also that he has challenged society's values and "God".

He kills her with "all her hair". The unexpected "all" implies that her hair has disgusted him. She's used it to try to seduce him, but also to cover his head and face. It is a symbol of all the ways she feels superior to him.

He is able to wind her hair into a string, which is a slow and dominant action, suggesting that Porphyria allows this, welcoming his change in sexual behaviour. This is also emphasised by how she appears to give him time to wind it around her neck three times before she realises the danger.

"And strangled her" is a surprising line, which is also heightened by how short it is. It shocks us and reminds us of the shock Porphyria must have felt.

His description of her death is signposted as untrustworthy. He repeats she felt "no pain" as though to persuade himself this is true. This makes us doubt that in death she is still "smiling" and that her eyes still "laughed".

Then, finally, it challenges us to look at the final line, where "God has not said a word". It is easy to see this as pure self-deception – Browning's overwhelmingly Christian readers would choose this view.

But another possibility is the secrecy of this affair. Porphyria has indeed kept him secret, in a cottage, unseen by others. There will be no evidence to say who she met there. This is perhaps another reason why we never find out the name of Porphyria's lover: he is able to remain anonymous, and will never be brought to justice. Viewed in this way, his confession taunts the reader.

He confesses without fear of being caught, and refuses to feel guilt. This challenges us to ask if God really will punish him, or if, as the lover appears to believe, God is "silent" because he is absent.

Alfred Lord Tennyson (1809 to 1892)

Look, you won't use much of this in an essay. But some of it will just come to you as you write an essay, and it will get you up a grade, because you will link it to the author's purpose. And knowing stuff just makes you cleverer! It isn't just about Tennyson, and will help you understand the Victorians more fully.

Tennyson was the most famous poet of the 1800s in a time when that meant fame. His books of poetry would sell 17,000 copies on one day.

Tennyson: Young, Beautiful, Clever

Like Blake, Wordsworth and Shelley, he began writing poetry as a boy, as a passion. His father was a church rector who had to support 11 children, so there was no private school for Tennyson. He was bullied at grammar school, and so left to be educated at home by his father. This would have been interesting, as his father was both an alcoholic and a drug user.

Like Shelley, he went to Oxbridge – attending Trinity in Cambridge. In 1827, his first poetry book was published with his brothers, and his first solo book in 1830, **Poems, Chiefly Lyrical**. We can see that he was passionate about the sounds words make, and the rhythms of poetry, which you will see in **The Charge of the Light Brigade**.

He was very handsome as well as a brilliant poet, and immediately gained the attention of a group of students who called themselves The Apostles, which included the most gifted student of his time, Arthur Hallam.

Like Shelley, Tennyson did not complete his degree. For Tennyson it was because his father died in 1830, and money was tight.

Tennyson and Politics

In the summer of 1830 Tennyson and Hallam travelled to the Pyrenees to give money and messages to revolutionaries plotting the overthrow of the Spanish king. We can see Tennyson trying to find a political voice like Shelley and Blake, but he realized these revolutionaries were simply self-interested, rather than fighting for ideals.

He rejected radical politics as a subject of his poetry, and rather than write poetry of protest, he took to supporting his country patriotically and politically, as we will later see in **The Charge of the Light Brigade.**

The landscape here captivated him, just as mountainous landscapes captivated Shelley and Wordsworth. He returned to the village of Cauteretz many times, and it inspired many of his poems, notably **The Lotus Eaters** and **The Eagle**.

Poetry and Art

Perhaps surprisingly for a modern audience, writing poetry was seen as a manly and a noble pursuit. Art was considered much more than entertainment, or the expression of novelty as it is today. Art and poetry were seen as ways to uncover truths about mankind and nature – truths which were considered eternal, rather than rooted in any one historical time.

To express these truths in exactly the right words, in ways that everyone could understand them, was considered a wonderful skill. If you have ever memorised a poem, you will know what I mean – it comes back to you again and again. You will find times where individual phrases come back to you because they are suddenly relevant to what you are experiencing.

Poetry was not difficult, or tucked away in GCSE exams, never to be seen again. People read it for pleasure, and turned to it in times of stress, sorrow, grief, love and joy.

Any educated person would have memorised numerous poems in the same way in which you have memorised dozens of songs. It's a very rare song which crafts language like a poem does, though sometimes a line like "I set fire to the rain" will stay with me forever, in the same way that a sand dune always reminds me of "the lone and level sands" and that Shelley had obviously never seen the Sahara desert, was factually totally wrong, and yet writing about the truth of time in a way which has deeper meaning as you get older.

Poems grow with you, like planting a tree, and they give people shade long after the poet has died.

Knowing this will help you see the poets' purposes in a different way – their poems were conversations with readers who were not just interested, but passionate. They believed in art as noble and truthful, and above all beautiful.

I'm not saying you have to think of art this way – but knowing that Victorians did will help you write about the poet's intentions and the effect on the contemporary reader.

Tennyson, the Poor Poet

The writers we study were much closer to tragedy than we are today, and I say that as someone who has been bankrupt, homeless for a year and a half, an illegal immigrant, deported, and moved around nine different schools.

The Poetry Foundation has this to say of Tennyson: "Part of the family heritage was a strain of epilepsy, a disease then thought to be brought on by sexual excess and therefore shameful. One of Tennyson's brothers was confined to an insane asylum most of his life, another had recurrent bouts of addiction to drugs, a third had to be put into a mental home because of his alcoholism, another was intermittently confined and died relatively young. Of the rest of the eleven children who reached maturity, all had at least one severe mental breakdown."

In 1832 he published another book of poetry which received bad reviews, and though he kept writing, he refused to publish for another ten years.

His best friend, Arthur Hallam, was engaged to Tennyson's sister and died in 1833. Tennyson wrote his most famous collection of poems, **In Memoriam**, to deal with his grief. In 1850 he published it, at first privately, and it led to him becoming the great superstar of Victorian poetry.

Like Pip, in **Great Expectations**, Tennyson fell in love with a woman whose family was too wealthy for him to marry into, Rosa Baring.

Then in 1836 he fell in love with Emily Sellwood, and became engaged. However, his family had a history of epilepsy, and Tennyson feared he would pass this on to his children, so refused to get married, ending the engagement in 1840.

Like Blake, who had had childhood visions, Tennyson had a history of entering into trances, which he assumed were signs of epilepsy.

In 1842 he finally published another book of poetry, but at the same time lost nearly all his money investing in a business which collapsed.

In 1845 an insurance payout recovered some of his losses.

In 1847 he published **The Princess**, a long poem calling for the education of women. We don't see any reference to the patriarchy in **The Charge of the Light Brigade**, but it will be a useful piece of historical knowledge when you consider what Browning might be saying about the patriarchal society, or indeed Dickens and Stevenson.

Tennyson, Famous Superstar

This book was a huge success and led to Queen Victoria appointing him poet laureate. Perhaps we might expect a queen to be determined to improve the education of women. He also married Emily that year, in 1850, once he discovered that he did not have epilepsy. In 1852 they had their first son, named Hallam after his best friend.

In Memoriam, published in 1850, was a collection of poems centred on grief, death and how to cope with it, inspired largely by his relationship with Hallam. Other big themes included the big questions Victorians were struggling with at the time:

Charles Lyell's Principles of Geology, published 1830-33 showed the earth was millions of years old, and this was the first of the many scientific challenges to the truth of the Bible.

You can see how this caused Christians to be anxious long before the publication of Darwin's theory of evolution.

Desperate to follow the Romantic tradition of Wordsworth, the previous poet laureate, Tennyson wore the same inaugural clothes which Wordsworth had worn. We can see the romantic influence on his poetry with an obsession with the middle ages in one of his most famous poems, **The Lady of Shallot**.

At this point he became internationally famous, and increasingly sought peace and quiet. In 1853, he moved to The Isle of Wight. Here his visitors included Prince Albert (Victoria's husband), and the queen of Hawaii. Queen Victoria also had a home on The Isle of Wight.

Why is all this important?

Here we can see Tennyson becoming part of the establishment. From his poor, uncertain upbringing, we can also imagine the huge attraction of protecting the establishment, which must have motivated him to celebrate even military failure in **The Charge of the Light**

Brigade, which he wrote in 1854. This is doubly important because this was a rare war in which Britain's victory felt like a loss to many people at home.

In 1859 he published the first of four books about King Arthur, **Idyll's of the King**. (This, I suggest, is a major reason why Priestley calls Birling 'Arthur', as you may have read in my **Mr Salles Guide to An Inspector Calls**).

This continued the romantic tradition of his predecessors, and tapped into the contemporary fascination with the gothic. However, it also focuses on a mythical England which was united and noble.

One way of looking at this is as a parallel to the creation of Empire. Victorians didn't just export trade across the world, but took over dozens of countries in order to spread what they saw as British values – law, government and Christianity. They did not see themselves as invaders, but makers of a better world. If you understand that, you can see why they might think that war against Russia in a part of the Ukraine near Turkey was any of our business in the first place!

The Charge of the Light Brigade, by Alfred Lord Tennyson

I

Half a league, half a league,

Half a league onward,

All in the valley of Death

Rode the six hundred.

"Forward, the Light Brigade!

Charge for the guns!" he said.

Into the valley of Death

Rode the six hundred.

II

"Forward, the Light Brigade!"

Was there a man dismayed?

Not though the soldier knew

Someone had blundered.

Theirs not to make reply,

Theirs not to reason why,

Theirs but to do and die.

Into the valley of Death

Rode the six hundred.

III

Cannon to right of them,

Cannon to left of them,

Cannon in front of them

Volleyed and thundered;

Stormed at with shot and shell,

Boldly they rode and well,

Into the jaws of Death,
Into the mouth of hell
Rode the six hundred.

IV

Flashed all their sabres bare,
Flashed as they turned in air
Sabring the gunners there,
Charging an army, while
All the world wondered.
Plunged in the battery-smoke
Right through the line they broke;
Cossack and Russian
Reeled from the sabre stroke
Shattered and sundered.
Then they rode back, but not
Not the six hundred.

V

Cannon to right of them,
Cannon to left of them,
Cannon behind them
Volleyed and thundered;
Stormed at with shot and shell,
While horse and hero fell.
They that had fought so well
Came through the jaws of Death,
Back from the mouth of hell,
All that was left of them,

Left of six hundred.

VI

When can their glory fade?

O the wild charge they made!

All the world wondered.

Honour the charge they made!

Honour the Light Brigade,

Noble six hundred!

Context and Tennyson's Purpose

The Crimean War was a rare British war, because although the Russians negotiated for peace, the British lost 25,000 men, most of them to cold and disease, and it felt a bit like a defeat. Tennyson read about the charge on the 2nd of December 1854 in The Times newspaper, and published the poem on 9th of December. This was the first fully reported war, complete with photographs, and news wired in by telegraph, so that news, for the first time in history, travelled fast.

So this poem is written as propaganda to build public support for the war.

Tennyson wrote it to persuade the country that the costly war would still reveal British greatness. It is a patriotic poem, celebrating the Victorian drive to expand the Empire.

Tennyson's Propaganda

Although he may have doubted his own Christian faith, he deliberately used biblical allusions to suit his audience's Christian tastes. "The valley of death" is a quotation from Psalm 23, which his readers would probably know by heart. The next part of the line is "though I walk through the valley of the shadow of death, I will fear no evil: for thou *(meaning God)* art with me." Tennyson wants his readers to see the war as a just war.

More importantly, he wants them to see the "blunder" as a consequence of war, rather than incompetence. Instead of blaming the officer who gave the order, it is only a nameless "someone" who is to blame. God, the allusion implies, will welcome the souls of all those who died.

British Heroism

He uses metonymy, replacing "The Light Brigade" with "the six hundred". Tennyson does this both to suggest that hundreds were killed, but also that the charge against impossible odds was carried out by very few men. It emphasises the logical conclusion the men must have made – that death was nearly inevitable, but that they would follow orders anyway.

To prove this, we only have to look at how much easier it is to rhyme with "brigade" than it is with "hundred". But the difficulty was worth it, because he wanted to show how many men had died heroically.

He celebrates the British soldier who will follow this order, even if it ends in certain death, "Theirs but to do and die". The "and" makes very clear that death is inevitable, but duty and patriotism is more important.

Structure and Grammar

He shows the overwhelming force of the Russians through grammatical choice, where they charge with "Cannon to right of them", rather than to 'the' right. This implies that they are everywhere on the right. The trick is repeated with "Cannon to left of them" so that rather than simply facing cannons on both sides, it sounds as though they are completely surrounded.

Another reason, of course, is the rhythm created by six syllables, instead of seven. It also allows every third syllable to be stressed, creating a rhythm like hoofbeats, mimicking the sound of the charge.

A final way he uses this line is to echo it at the end of the poem, where he repeats "left". The survivors are described as "All that was left of them, / Left of six hundred". Perhaps this implies a deeper dissatisfaction with the war itself. Although the poem is in praise of the soldiers and their "noble" sacrifice, he may still believe the sacrifice is not "right". The repetition of "left" reminds us of the missing "right". Perhaps their deaths were wrong.

The Rhyme Scheme

Tennyson's use of rhyme is very revealing. Let's look at the beginning.

"Forward, the Light **Brigade**!" (A)
Was there a man **dismayed**? (A)
Not though the soldier **knew** (B)
Someone had **blundered**. (C)
Theirs not to make **reply**, (D)
Theirs not to reason **why**, (D)
Theirs but to do and **die**. (D)
Into the valley of **Death** (E)
Rode the six **hundred**." (C)

We can see that the pattern is disrupted – we would expect the last two lines to be a rhyming couplet, like the opening two lines. But he doesn't give us this neat ending, because the meeting of "the six hundred" with "Death" is not a neat ending.

Despite the celebratory tone of the poem, Tennyson implies that it is unacceptable. The other non-rhyming line is "though the soldier knew". Ending with this enjambment shows how certain this knowledge is, that an officer "had blundered" in condemning them to charge towards death.

Rather than celebrating this order with rhyme, to emphasise the soldier's heroism, he contrasts that heroism with the blunder – the line itself mimics a blunder, failing to rhyme. Tennyson makes this point doubly clear with the half rhyme of "hundred" and "blundered", emphasising the blunder again.

The verses are also written in dactyls, which is what we call three syllables, only the first of which is stressed. Here's what it looks like with the stressed syllables in bold:

"**For**ward, the **Light** Brigade!"
Was there a **man** dismayed?
Not though the **sol**dier knew
Someone had **blun**dered.
Theirs not to **make** reply,
Theirs not to **reas**on why,
Theirs but to **do** and die.

So, how can we relate this to the meaning of the poem? The rhythm Dum da da Dum da da gives it a light-hearted beat, like a song. Try reading it out loud like this, and it simply feels wrong. It only really works if you sing it. When you read it, you'll also emphasise other syllables.

(Try singing it to the tune of 'Let's go Fly a Kite' from Mary Poppins, and you'll see what I mean).

Perhaps Tennyson does this to point out the irony of his own poem, that he is celebrating the extraordinary bravery of great men, but whose sacrifice and death was utterly pointless, reflected in the cheerful rhythm.

The Sounds of the Poem

Astonishingly, Tennyson recorded himself reading the poem in his 80s, and you can find this on the internet. Although he appears to follow the stresses of the dactyls, he deviates from it dramatically on "knew".

This reinforces the likelihood that he wants to criticise the "blunder". He can't do this explicitly in a patriotic poem which celebrates the British military, but a reader attuned to sound would certainly spot the discord, where the dactyl rhythm is deliberately disrupted.

Tennyson plays with sound in other ways. He uses anaphora to describe the surrounding cannons, "Cannon to right of them / Cannon to left of them / Cannon in front of them." The repetition at the beginning of the line emphasises the number of cannons, but also that they are inescapable, which suggests the Light Brigade will be lucky to survive. This in turn emphasises their bravery and sense of duty, which makes them "noble" in Tennyson's eyes.

Alliteration is used to make the poem memorable – it is easy to overlook that memorising poems was a source of joy to Victorian readers.

Tennyson also uses it to emphasise mood. The alliteration of w in "while/All the world wondered" tells the reader to be filled with awe, as the first meaning of wonder here suggests the whole world is filled with wonder, because the soldiers' courage and loyalty is so great.

However, the secondary reading involves emphasises wondered as a question. The alliterative w's remind us of the earlier "why". The soldiers did not "reason why", but Tennyson subtly invites his discerning reader to question why.

It is important to realise that the first meaning is front and centre, because on the surface this is a deeply patriotic poem, that does not want to criticise the military or the purpose of the war against Russia, which the British saw as a just cause.

Similarly, Tennyson also subtly criticises this view with his rhyme scheme. "Russian" is another word which Tennyson refuses to rhyme, as though it is misplaced in the stanza. This might imply that the war with Russia is itself out of place. The British are not fighting a war to defend its own territories, they have simply joined as allies in someone else's war.

The Ottoman Empire (Turkey) had attacked Russia, and Britain felt it had to defend the Turks in order to preserve overland trade with India.

It's not much of a rallying cry, is it, 'let's fight to the death to defend our overland trade route with India, because our ships aren't going to make us quite as much money, as they take a little bit longer to get there'.

But remember, he can't say this directly, as this would be deeply unpatriotic and wouldn't fit his role as Poet Laureate.

A final possibility is that Tennyson was not even aware of his own misgivings, that they are unconscious and not fully formed, and are simply revealed by his rhyme scheme. That id getting its way without the ego noticing! But I don't buy that. A poet who works at rhyme would be deeply irritated by lines which didn't. He would only keep them if they served a greater purpose.

Poetry Exam Tactics

There are two boxes you must tick in order to get into the top band – the **'form'** box, and the **'structure'** box.

Most modern poets couldn't give a rat's whatsit about the form of their poem, unless they are very deliberately echoing a classical form, such as a sonnet, or a ballad. Sadly, our poets ain't.

This means that, in theory, you can't get full marks if you aren't commenting on a pre 20th century poem. So, study these! They are the key to top grades.

Exam Technique: The FOSSE Way

Ok, now you have an in depth understanding of the poems I've covered which is much greater than you could possibly use in the exam. That's why I love to teach. But many of you won't want to study English Literature at A level, and just want to pass the exam, thank you very much.

So I confess, to pass the exam, you need to know very little.

1. The poet's purpose is everything – you want to know why she or he wrote the poem, and better still, have more than one reason.
2. Then you have to compare it to another poem. This is not a Literature skill. It isn't something you do at university, it is a made up GCSE exam skill. So the trick is to find a poem that deals with similar themes and ideas.
3. Then you have to choose the best bits to compare. In reality, these could come from any part of the poem. But, because you want this to link to the poet's purpose, you will find the parts of the poem which set out the poet's purpose – the beginning – and the bit which gives a final perspective on that purpose – the ending.
4. Next you have to consider the other parts of the mark scheme, which talk about methods, form and structure. So, you need to compare all three of those as well.
5. That means a total of 5 comparisons: beginning, some sort of poetic technique, something about the structure, something else about the form (or type of poem), and something about the ending.
6. Here's a handy mnemonic to help you remember:

Form
Opening
SOAPAIMS
Structure
Ending

FOSSE? Well, it will have to do. Email me a better one if you have it. I used to drive to school on the longest and oldest Roman road in Britain. It is called The Fosse Way. So there you have it, the FOSSE way of comparing poems. It's Roman. It will stand the test of time!

And for each of those five comparisons you must try to relate that to the poet's purposes.

What Should My Essay Look Like?

If you follow the **FOSSE Way**, you can see that you would have 10 paragraphs.

1. Paragraph 1, the **F**orm and purpose of poem 1.
2. Paragraph 2, compare to the Form and purpose of poem 2.
3. Paragraph 3, the **O**pening and purpose of poem 1.
4. Paragraph 4, compare to the Opening and purpose of poem 2.
5. Paragraph 5, compare the poetic techniques (**S**OAPAIMS) and purpose in poem 1.
6. Paragraph 6, compare the poetic techniques (SOAPAIMS) and purpose in poem 2.
    (In practice I tend to find that this analysis of poetic techniques forces me to write about structure as well, at the same time. This can reduce your number of paragraphs).
7. Paragraph 7, analyse **S**tructure and relate it to purpose in poem 1.
8. Paragraph 8, analyse Structure and relate it to purpose in poem 2.
9. Paragraph 9, analyse the **E**nding and relate to final purpose in poem 1.
10. Paragraph 10, analyse the Ending and relate to final purpose in poem 2.

This will 100% work, and can give you a grade 9.

However, this isn't how you would write a comparison or an essay at A level, or at university. So, if you want to deviate from this, you can, so long as you write a range of comparisons and cover all the 5 elements above.

Compare War Photographer and Charge of the Light Brigade.

There are many themes that could be chosen in a question on power and conflict.

How do the poets present their ideas about:

1. War
2. The effects of war on the participants
3. The imagery of war
4. The effects of war on the public
5. Duty in times of conflict
6. The power of newspapers
7. Public opinion about war
8. Heroism
9. Fighting foreign wars

10. Poetry about war is political

In reality, even the least able student in your school has to have a chance at answering the question, so the examiners will ask a broad and bland question about 'the effects of war'. This means that you can write about anything, and 4 to 10 above are your best bets, because they are all about the poet's purpose.

Compare How the Poets Present the Effects of War in War Photographer and One Other Poem, Using the FOSSE Way

Form

Duffy wants to bring out the horror of foreign war to force us to face up to the suffering we read about and see in the news, so that we will take some responsibility in changing our support for those wars. Consequently, she chooses to disrupt the pattern of rhyming couplets, and a syllable pattern which refuses to settle. This is a poem designed both to be memorable, and to unsettle us.

Tennyson also writes about a foreign war, reported in the news, taking his inspiration from an article in the Times which most of his readers would have read only the week before his publication. He has a specific war, the Crimea, in mind, and writes to persuade his readers to support the war out of a patriotic duty which is mirrored by the heroic sense of duty displayed by the Light Brigade, despite heavy loss of life in "The Valley of Death". However, he too disrupts the rhyming form of his poem, so that we are unsettled by the "blunder" of the charge and perhaps even by our entry to the war itself.

Opening

Duffy begins her poem with a Christian allusion, in an ironic simile, as though her war photographer is "a priest preparing to intone a Mass". This reminds us deliberately of eternal life, which is being denied to those being killed in the rest of the poem, implying that war is an anti-Christian act. She follows immediately with an allusion to the Old Testament, "all flesh is grass" which points out both that life is brief, and our lives are cut short like "grass", but also that it is sacred, a gift from God.

Tennyson also uses Christian allusion to reach his audience with a reference all his readers would know, and most would have memorised by heart. "The Valley of Death" paraphrases Psalm 23, "though I walk through the valley of the shadow of death, I will fear no evil, for thou art with me". This implies that the soldiers die at God's side, and though dead in this life, are immediately welcomed to heaven. This portrays war as just and Christian, the opposite of Duffy's point. However, "Death" ends the rhyme without rhyming, and consequently jars the rhythm of the poem. Tennyson's more subtle point might be that the patriotic propaganda of his poem is just a veneer, and that death in this war is both tragic and anti-Christian.

SOAPAIMS with a bit of Structure

Duffy drums home her political point with an alliterative list of foreign conflicts which took place at a precise time, the 1970s, "Belfast. Beirut. Phnom Penh". Significantly, she begins with a British war in "Belfast" against Catholics, and then each foreign war becomes greater in scale, ending with mass slaughter in Cambodia where political rulers exterminated 20% of their own population. British readers would be familiar with this horror, but also become immune to it, as Duffy describe them, and us, turning to "pre-lunch beers". She therefore blames us. Her reference to "Belfast" blames our government, and its consequent support of American wars is blamed with "Phnom Penh".

SOAPAIMS

Tennyson also focuses on a historical moment, but his purpose is the opposite. He wants to focus on the "Noble six hundred" who do their duty in war, no matter the personal cost to themselves. Their duty is "but to do and die" for their country. Consequently, he presents them as heroic, rather than mindless. He also uses a list, through anaphora, "Cannon to right of them/ Cannon to left of them/ Cannon behind them". The repetition of "Cannon" emphasises the superior fire power of the "Cossak and Russian" in contrast to the Light Brigade charging only with "sabres". Tennyson omits "the" in to the left, and to the right, to suggest that they are surrounded by "Cannon", implying that only a miracle will help them escape "the jaws of Death".

Structure

He also does this to preserve the dactylic rhythm he chooses for the poem. The dactyls stress the first syllable, while the next two die away. This recreates the rhythm of a song, highlighting the purpose of the poem, to celebrate British heroism. However, Tennyson also subtly attacks the officer who "blundered". Although all his readers would have read in the news that this was Lord Raglan, Tennyson writes in his role as poet laureate, supporting the establishment, so he only states "someone had blundered" which "the soldier knew".

Furthermore, this last dactyl should stress the first syllable of "soldier". However, Tennyson disrupts that by stressing "knew". Again he emphasises this disruption by refusing to rhyme. This is deliberate, as we can hear in his own reading of the poem, where he stresses "knew" at the end of the dactyl. The knowledge he wants to emphasise is that the charge, and perhaps the Crimean war itself, was a terrible mistake.

Ending

Both poems end with a focus on the future. Duffy ends accusing the readers of newspapers: "they do not care". The use of "they" invites us to see them as different from us, because she is inviting us to agree that the poem has changed us "to do what someone must" like the photographer, to bear witness to the horror of war and so campaign to stop it.

Tennyson does not ask his readers to protest against future wars. Instead, he asks rhetorically "When can their glory fade?" which implies that we will always glorify the sacrifice of our soldiers in future wars. Instead of focusing on the horror of war, we must "honour the Light Brigade", and support warfare. However, his final line typically undermines this, ending with "six hundred", another line which he refuses to rhyme.

Tennyson makes sure we are reminded of the first rhyme in this sequence – it was a half rhyme with "blundered". Consequently, his final line invites us to think more deeply about the blunder of the charge, and perhaps the "blunder" of the war itself.

986 Words

Full marks 30/30

Grade Boundaries

In 2018 students needed a relatively low score to gain a grade 6.

If you have got this far in reading the guide, I have no doubt you are easily able to get this grade.

All you need is 57%!

What does 57% mean in the mark scheme?

Your essay must score 17.1 out of 30!

Here are the skills that would earn you that mark in level 4

(16-20 marks):

Clear understanding

For 20 marks, a candidate's response is likely to be:

1. Clear, **sustained** and consistent.
2. **A focused comparison** which demonstrates clear understanding.
3. Using **a range of references** effectively to illustrate and justify explanation;
4. There will be clear explanation of the **effects of a range of writer's methods**
5. **Supported by** appropriate use of **subject terminology**.
6. Show a clear understanding of **ideas/perspectives/contextual factors**

Notice that there is no need to write about **form and structure** to get this mark! If you do write about form and structure, the examiner automatically has to consider you for a higher grade!!!!

(BTW, never use more than one exclamation mark, but I wanted to interrupt myself and write to you in ways you are more familiar with to point out how absolutely mind bogglingly brilliant this piece of information is. It tells you just how easy it is to get a good grade. True dat as we used to say in 2015).

Grade 7 is only 66%! This would be 20 marks out of 30. So you only need to write a tiny bit about structure or form to get 21 marks, which is going to be a proper grade 7! I know, right?

What are the extra skills of grade 7?

- The essay will be thoughtful
- Thoughtfully comparing methods
- Thoughtfully dealing with context.

Compare How the Poets Present the Effects of War in War Photographer and One Other Poem Grade 7

(Without writing about structure and form)

1. Duffy wants to bring out the horror of foreign war to force us to face up to the suffering we read about and see in the news. This is a poem designed both to be memorable, and to unsettle us.

2. Tennyson also writes about a foreign war, the Crimea. He wants to persuade his readers to admire the suffering and bravery of British soldiers, particularly the Light Brigade, who charge into "The Valley of Death" even though they know they will probably die.

3. Duffy compares the war photographer with a simile, so he is like "a priest preparing to intone a Mass". A priest is a Christian, and the reader knows that Christians should not kill. This is ironic as the photographer does not kill, but takes pictures of death. Duffy reminds us of how much death there is in war by linking this to a biblical reference, "all flesh is grass". This means that everyone's life can be cut short in war, so we can see how shocking war is.

4. Tennyson also makes a reference to the Bible. "The Valley of Death" comes from Psalm 23. This implies that God is on the same side as the British soldiers and though they will die, he will welcome them in heaven. It also suggests that the British are right to fight the Russians as Tennyson is telling us that God sides with "the Light Brigade".

5. Duffy gives her readers a list of violent foreign wars, "Belfast. Beirut. Phnom Penh". Belfast is the smallest conflict, and then they get bigger, with many more deaths. Perhaps she is suggesting that wars keep getting worse because the public don't do enough to protest. Instead, she says, the readers go back to their "pre-lunch beers" after they have seen wars in the news, and ignore the killing.

6. Tennyson doesn't focus on the killing. Instead he focuses on the soldiers' heroic deaths as they do their duty. He shows their heroism with the phrase "theirs but to do and die". He also uses anaphora to emphasise how brave they are. So they charge with "Cannon to right of them/ Cannon to left of them/ Cannon behind them". The repetition of "Cannon" emphasises the superior fire power of the "Cossak and Russian" in contrast to the Light Brigade charging only with "sabres". Tennyson shows us this so we can see their bravery.

7. Although readers at the time might have been critical of the order to charge, Tennyson doesn't want to attack the generals running the war. So he just states "someone had blundered" in giving the order to charge. This makes us focus on the bravery of the soldiers instead of focusing on the stupidity of the officers.

8. Both poets want to influence how we think about war. Duffy ends accusing the readers of newspapers: "they do not care". Using "they" to describe the reader

shows that Duffy wants us to be different, and to "care" about the "spools of suffering" we see in the news.

9. Tennyson wants us to always celebrate British soldiers, so he uses the rhetorical question "When can their glory fade?" This implies that their heroism was so great we should never forget them. Instead of thinking about the suffering of war, he wants us to remember the bravery of "the Light Brigade".

551 words

Go back over the paragraphs and work out which ones you think are "thoughtful". (Even English teachers might not agree on this, so just use a gut reaction).

My gut reaction is that 3, 4, 5, 6, 7 and 9 are all "thoughtful" comparisons.

Grade 6 Version

It is pretty difficult for me as a teacher to write an essay that would only get a grade 6, because it doesn't have to be "thoughtful". Here is my attempt at only being "clear".

The examiner's comment in is italics.

1. Duffy wants to bring out the horror of foreign war to force us to face up to the suffering we read about and see in the news. This is a poem designed both to be memorable, and to unsettle us.
   (Note there is more than one purpose)

2. Tennyson also writes about a foreign war, the Crimea. He wants to persuade his readers to admire the suffering and bravery of British soldiers, particularly the Light Brigade, who charge into "The Valley of Death" even though they know they will probably die.
   (Note there is more than one purpose)

3. Duffy compares the war photographer with a simile, so he is like "a priest preparing to intone a Mass". A priest is a Christian, and the reader knows that Christians should not kill. Duffy reminds us of how much death there is in war with the reference, "all flesh is grass". This means that everyone's life can be cut short in war, so we can see how shocking war is.
   (There are two parts to the explanation in PEE, with a clear link to the poet's purpose.)

4. Tennyson also makes a reference to the Bible with the "The Valley of Death." This implies that God is on their side and will welcome "the Light Brigade" into heaven when they die.
   (There is only one explanation in PEE, but it does link to literary context, and religious context)

5. Duffy gives her readers a list of violent foreign wars, "Belfast. Beirut. Phnom Penh". Belfast is the smallest war, and then they get bigger, with many more deaths. She wants us to be shocked by this. She attacks the readers because all they think about is their "pre-lunch beers" after they have seen wars in the news. They ignore the killing.
   (There are two parts to the explanation in PEE, clearly linked to the poet's purpose.)

6. Tennyson doesn't focus on the killing. Instead he focuses on the soldiers' heroic deaths as they do their duty. He shows their heroism with the phrase "theirs but to do and die". He also uses anaphora to show how brave they are, charging at the "Cannon to right of them/ Cannon to left of them/ Cannon behind them". However, "the Light Brigade" only have "sabres". Tennyson shows us this so we can see their bravery.
   (This paragraph is possibly slightly too good for grade 6 – it has more than one interpretation, plus great subject terminology, plus there is an alternative viewpoint – shown by 'however').

7. Tennyson didn't want his readers to blame the generals at the time for giving the order to charge. So he just states "someone had blundered" in giving the order to charge. This makes us focus on the bravery of the soldiers instead of focusing on the stupidity of the officers.
(This has two explanations and a clear link to the poet's purpose).

8. Both poets want to influence how we think about war. Duffy ends accusing the readers of newspapers: "they do not care". Using "they" to describe the reader shows that Duffy wants us to be different, and to "care" about the photographs of war we see in the news.
(Clear understanding of the poet's purpose.)

9. Tennyson wants us to always celebrate British soldiers, so he uses the rhetorical question "When can their glory fade?" This implies that their heroism was so great we should never forget them. Instead of thinking about the suffering of war, he wants us to remember the bravery of "the Light Brigade".
(Clear understanding of the poet's purpose.)

484 words

Go back and look at the previous essays to see why this is only **clear**, and not **focused** and **sustained**.

Here is another Grade 9 poetry comparison. For your revision, see if you can reduce it to the number of words you can write in 45 minutes.

Notice it is also about two 19th century poems – at least one of which you will probably be able to use in your exam, so it will also be worth memorising the points of this essay.

Essay: How do the poets present power in Ozymandias and London?

Both Blake and Shelley criticise the misuse of power by those superior in social hierarchy. Shelley and Blake, as romanticists, reacted against the restrictions of classical thought and countered many of the beliefs which existed within society.

Blake was a great believer in equality of man. This was largely due to his belief that God exists within everyone: we are all equal. Consequently, any form of power stemming from social hierarchy was corrupt and unjust. In 'London', Blake attacks established organisations (the church and royalty) for their misuse of power. Similarly, Shelley attacks Ozymandias, representing Ramesses II, for his tyranny and dictatorship.

Shelley imagines 'a traveller from an antique land', who describes the statue of Ozymandias as 'sunk' and 'shattered'. This suggests the shattering of Ozymandias' rule and the fragility of power which is 'sunk' over time. Perhaps Shelley is suggesting that the pursuit of fame and power is ultimately pointless, as time will eradicate all power and fame.

Furthermore, Shelley suggests that the dictator ruled with the 'sneer of cold command'. The alliteration of 'cold command' emphasises the emotionless nature of Ozymandias' rule. It suggests that Ozymandias ruled for his own benefit, sneering at his own people. As a romanticist, Shelley valued individuality and freedom of emotion. By using alliteration to highlight his 'cold command' perhaps Shelley is condemning Ozymandias for ruling without emotional thought for his people.

Like Shelley, Blake too criticises those in power, the church and royalty, for their treatment of people in their society. He uses soft sibilance ironically to describe the 'hapless soldiers sigh'. This contrast displays Blake's disgust at how soldiers are treated by the 'palace'. The 'sigh' may also indicate that the soldiers, without complaint, have succumbed to their fate: 'runs in blood down palace walls'. The 'palace walls' not only provide safety for those with money but they are symbolic of the segregation between those with power and the commoners walking the streets of London.

Furthermore, Blake criticises the 'church' using metaphorical language of the 'blackening church appals'. As the church was partially responsible for the 'chimney sweeper's cry', encouraging chimney sweeping, the word 'appals' condemns the church for their child cruelty. The church is 'blackening' as Blake views it as a soulless, deadly place, abusing its power and destroying the innocence of 'youth'.

Similarly to Blake, Shelley uses metaphorical language to describe 'the heart that fed'. This is a particularly gothic image as a 'heart' typically gives life. Instead, Ozymandias' heart is feeding on the people he has power over. This reading is supported by the use of 'stamped on...lifeless things'. The word 'stamped' is indicative of Ozymandias' abuse of power, suggesting that he ruled with force oppressing his people until they became literally or figuratively 'lifeless'.

Ozymandias subsequently seems to celebrate his absolute power, proclaiming to be the 'king of kings' and ordering us to 'look on my works...and despair'. Alternatively perhaps it is the 'sculptor' who is 'mocking' Ozymandias. The only thing that has partially survived in the 'level sands' is the sculptor's work. Therefore, 'Ye Mighty' could be read with a mocking tone as all that is left of Ozymandias' power and fame is the sculptor's art. Perhaps Shelley is suggesting that the power of art is more sustainable than an individual's power.

However, unlike Shelley, Blake suggests that the oppression in society is partially self-inflicted. We are not physically bound by the laws of society but rather mentally restricted. This creates a far deeper kind of restriction, perhaps one that is harder to escape from. Blake believes "in every cry of every man...the mind forg'd manacles I hear". The repetition of 'every' suggests a unity of emotion, everybody displays the same 'marks of weakness, marks of woe', even in the 'infant's cry'. This may suggest that children are born into a society which teaches oppression, shattering hope of childhood innocence and instead gifting them with 'mind-forged manacles'.

Interestingly, the idea that the 'manacles' are 'mind-forged' suggests that we are only restricted due to our own way of thinking and desire to conform to social norms. Perhaps Blake is suggesting that authority figures only have the power to oppress our individuality and freedom if we conform to perceived superiority. Therefore power is presented as subjective.

Blake ends 'London' with the oxymoron 'marriage hearse'. This could be his final attack on the power of the church. 'Marriage' is a sacred union, offered in the church and 'hearse' is associated with funerals. Perhaps Blake is suggesting that following holy rituals will not bring happiness and will instead end in misery and death.

Although this is a rather bleak ending to the poem, Shelley arguably ends Ozymandias more optimistically. He depicts 'level sands' which 'stretch far away'. As Shelley was extremely pro-democracy and wanted to change the government to become more democratic, 'level' could refer to the idea of democracy which is now present, even in 'far away' lands.

This idea of power becoming more 'level' is reflected in the structure of the poem. The poem changes from a Petrarchan sonnet, to a Shakespearian sonnet and ends without rhyme. This change in structure reflects the changing nature of power, which Shelley hopes will ultimately end in democracy. However, the lack of rhyme at the end of the poem may imply ambiguity: Shelley is uncertain of the political outcome of his 'land'.

In conclusion, Blake suggests that social hierarchy creates an imbalance of power. He suggests that whilst the church and royals abuse power, we are the cause of our own oppression as we conform to society's norms. Like Blake, Shelley too suggests that those in authority abuse power. However, Shelley is more optimistic by suggesting that the power of time and art will succeed the power of any individual.

959 words

Examiner's Comments

Although this student has very sustained comparisons, with plenty of interpretations, she nearly didn't get all the marks.

The paragraph in bold is the one that deals with 'form'. As you can see, because she doesn't have the exam criteria in her head, she nearly missed this. She realises this towards the end of the essay. Alarm bells ring!

(Mr Salles says: But perhaps your alarm bells won't ring. So deal with form early on. That's why the FOSSE Way works. Analyse 'form' first, and you have already planted a seed in the examiner's mind – "Ooh, this might be grade 7 or better.")

Naturally, she is able to write about a huge range of points because she is able to combine her quotation and explanation in the same sentence: she writes in PEE sentences. PEE paragraphs would have slowed her down.

(Mr Salles says: yes, if you are good enough, the FOSSE Way isn't necessary. If you are going to take A level, the FOSSE Way will be a little clunky and you will have to unlearn it. That is because comparing poems is not an English Literature skill, it is just invented by Ofqual for this exam. Yes, the exams actually make you worse at literature in this respect.)

Because she is able to write at grade 7 very comfortably, she doesn't have to rely on a method for the comparison. She knows she can write about one poem for a few paragraphs, and then compare to the second poem when she is ready.

How to Choose Poems to Compare

Grade 5 and 6, *Clear Comparisons*

Probably the most popular way to choose which poems to compare is to pick them by topic – those that are about war, or people in crisis, or romantic love, love between friends or family, those about nature, or a love of place, or the past, etc.

You can plan these in advance.

I'm giving you the extra tip of trying to use a 19th century poem, as this will also allow you to write about "form and structure" more easily, and push you towards, or into grade 7.

Grade 7, 8 and 9, *"Thoughtful Comparison"*

But this is a poor way to choose poems where you make thoughtful comparisons. They are instead pretty obvious comparisons.

Remember, you are trying to show the examiner your understanding of the writer's ideas. So, it is much more interesting to pick poems which are linked by idea. Ideas are, of course, thoughtful.

For example, **Kamikaze** is a poem about how a family deals with the after effect of war. **War Photographer** is about how a photographer and the general public deal with the after effects of war. **Remains** is about how a soldier deals with the after effects of war. So, either of these three will compare on subject matter.

So these are all clear comparisons – the after effect of war.

But, this ignores the writer's ideas. To say that war has an after effect is not really an idea, it is like saying, 'because today is Friday, you are probably looking forward to the weekend.' Well, duh.

Let's Look at Some Ideas

Start with the ideas of one of the poems.

Kamikaze explores the ideas of a culture which celebrates loyalty to *higher ideals*, like *patriotism*, and *self-sacrifice*. The society in the poem has a *cult of death* which is more powerful than *love*.

If I have to choose a war poem (because the question might use the word "war") the better choice is now **Poppies**.

In **Poppies** it is the *cult of patriotism* that has taken the mother's son to war. This was more important to the son than his *love of life, or love of family*.

Poet's Purpose (which is their Idea)

Now I can contrast the mother's grief at his death with the kamikaze pilot's family's grief at their father and husband's survival, and I can ask if they are both anti-war poems, or do they argue that a culture is worth dying for?

But, if the word 'war' is not in the title, but 'conflict' is, then I might choose **My Last Duchess.**

Here the *self-sacrifice* is the wife's, both the original Duchess as his wife, and the Count's daughter, his next wife. Here the *ideal is not patriotism, but patriarchy* and satisfying male power. They have to satisfy both the Duke, and their fathers, who have arranged the marriage.

The *cult of subservience to male power* is preserved through the Duke's patronage of artists, all men, who portray women in subservient ways.

Poet's Purpose (which is their Idea)

Now I ask if both poems are critical of the society they describe, and if they both want to change ideals of manhood? Is the Duke's killing of his wife the same as Japanese society's killing of its pilots?

This will obviously make your essay much more original than other students.

Don't Forget the Superpower of Form

But it has an extra superpower. Remember, the top grades demand that you write about "form". Good luck in saying something meaningful about the form of Kamikaze or Poppies! But a 19th century poem will always have a form, and you will always be able to link the poet's choice of form to the meaning of the poem or our understanding of the poet's ideas.

What's the least you can revise?

When I analyse any of the poems, I will focus on only about 4 or 5 quotations. This will limit the amount you revise. When I give you notes, they may be detailed, so that you become expert in these 5 quotations. It means that you can use them to answer any question.

I hope you can see, when you use the FOSSE Way, 4 quotations is all you need, though it pays to have a 5th as insurance.

- You know that one has to be from the beginning,
- And one from the end.
- A further one must be a poetic technique.
- Another must link to the structure. It will also be another poetic technique.
- That's 4. Your fifth will be one you have most to say about in each poem. Inevitably, it will be either a poetic technique, or an example of structure, or from the beginning or end.

The Unseen Poem

This is a gift of a question, because most students are running out of steam now. This is a 2 hour and 15 minute exam, the longest one you take. Stamina is key here. Because you are marked compared to everyone else, it is here that you are able to get ahead of most students.

How to Plan Your Answer to Get Grades 5 and 6

If you don't already get grade 7 when you practise this question, you will have great success with this method:

1. Read the poem once, just to get the gist of it.
2. *Place a tick on the page.*
3. Read the poem again, to read for meaning.
4. *Place another tick on the page.*
5. Read the poem again to find which quotations you are going to use.
6. *Place another tick on the page.*

This has a huge advantage if you normally do this question badly. It means you will understand most or all of the poem, and you will know exactly what quotations to write about.

Because you don't start answering the question *till you can count three ticks on your page*, you won't cheat yourself by starting early and writing gibberish.

This only works if you spend 3-4 minutes on this: any more than that and you lose writing time.

AQA 24 marks! That means you have about 34 minutes to write your answer.

How Will You be Marked?

The assessment criteria for this is exactly the same as for the Modern Texts, except you don't have to give convincing interpretations.

This is a big clue, by the way, that you need context in all the other questions, as these give you convincing interpretations.

As the poems are unseen, you have no context.

The 6 Things You Must Do

1. Have a well structured argument.
2. It is therefore conceptualised, as you prove the argument through the whole essay
3. Use a range of judicious references.
4. Have an analysis of language which is insightful
5. and analyse both form and structure
6. Use judicious subject terminology.

Unseen Poem

Boy or Girl , by Dominic Salles

They say, what do you want,

A boy or a girl?

And I say, yes.

They say, what do you want?

And I say, a baby.

They say, what do you want,

A girl or a boy?

And I say, I want it to be healthy.

They say, you can't call it it.

They ask what clothes we've bought you,

Blue or pink?

And I say, we've stored up

So much love

It's spilling over everywhere.

We've bought you a chest of drawers

To put it in – I'm not sure

There will be room for clothes.

In '**Boy or Girl**' how does the poet present the speaker's attitude to having a baby?

[24 marks]

35 minutes

What the examiner is looking for:

Indicative content:

Examiners are encouraged to reward any valid interpretations. Answers might, however, include some of the following:

1. Explain how the speaker's* voice, perspective or **tone** helps us understand their **ideas and feelings**

2. Explain how the form **or structural features** help us understand the speaker's ideas or feelings
3. Explain how the **poetic techniques**, especially *metaphor, simile, alliteration, personification, sibilance* help us understand the speaker's ideas or feelings
4. Explain how the choice of **vocabulary**, the semantic field, creates the **tone** of the speaker, so that we understand their ideas and feelings.

*(You may get a poem where the speaker is not the poet, and the poet may therefore have created a speaker they disagree with. If you spot this, write about it! Many Simon Armitage and Carol Ann Duffy poems are like this. However, because even the least academic student in your class needs a sporting chance of answering the question, this is unlikely.)

The FOSSE Way

You will still use the FOSSE Way, because it will satisfy all the marking criteria.

Form

The form of the poem is a reported conversation in which the speaker is addressing their unborn child, revealed in the direct address, "we've bought you", at the end of the poem. It feels like a letter the child will read as they grow up, so the parent knows it will act as a kind of promise to the child.

Opening

The poem opens with a joke, where the speaker replies to the question of whether they want "a boy or a girl?" by answering the question with "yes". The repeated question asked by "they" and answered by "I" suggests that the speaker is in opposition to his or her questioners. Perhaps his tone suggests that these questioners represent society – it is social views which determine whether a parent would prefer a "boy or girl".

SOAPAIMS

The poem uses only one example of figurative language, with the metaphor "we've stored up/ So much love/ It's spilling over everywhere." The speaker ironically does this because their literal answers have not satisfied the questioners. Instead, the metaphor works as an analogy, to illustrate that parenting should be about "love". The speaker imagines waiting for a baby as an opportunity to "store" love, so much that it transforms everything in the parents' lives. This sense of plenty is conveyed in "spilling over everywhere".

A further possibility is that the speaker refuses to be drawn on the gender of the child because they don't want the child to have to conform to gender stereotypes of "pink" and "blue", male and female. Instead the "chest of drawers" suggests great storage is needed for what are only baby clothes. This implies it will probably contain clothes of both colours, and therefore of both genders, in order to need such large storage.

Structure

It is structured in the form of question and answer, in order for the speaker to prove a point, that "love" for the unborn baby is unconditional, doesn't depend on its gender, and is perhaps overwhelming.

Ending

The final metaphor also implies that the speaker has stopped worrying about whether their family or wider society will understand. Instead, the poet turns to direct address, "we've bought you", so that the new child will understand that parental love is unconditional, no matter what their sex.

The final lines, "I'm not sure/ There will be room for clothes" also implies that the real preparations parents need to make are not in practical matters, like making sure a room is ready for the baby, and that it has all the material things it needs.

Instead, the overwhelming need is not just "love", but unconditional love, which doesn't judge, and doesn't ask the child to conform to what the parent wants it to be, and instead rejoices in a new human being.

451 words

(Full marks, Grade 9)

Examiner's Comments

This fully explores the tone of the speaker, looking at vocabulary, figurative language and form and structure to explain how we understand the speaker's ideas and feelings.

It begins with a thesis, which is argued in each paragraph of the essay. It writes about the whole text, so the argument is fully developed.

The essay doesn't rely on paragraphs which always follow a PEE structure – sometimes the point, evidence and explanation are all contained in a single sentence, so the essay is able to make a wide range of points.

What Does a Grade 6 Essay Look Like?

Grade 6: Clear Understanding

1. It needs to be **clear** – so paragraphed, with connectives. The paragraphs have to be in a logical order.
2. Written in properly punctuated sentences, which make sense.
3. It has to be **sustained**, so at least 300 words long.
4. It has to be **focused** – so always using quotations and examples to back up points.
5. It needs a **range of references**, so at least 4 quotations.
6. It needs to **justify explanation**, so always using words like 'implies' and 'suggests'

7. It must have some accurate **subject terminology**.

(In bold are the words which are likely to appear in the mark scheme.)

Grade 6 Answer

No Form

The poem feels as though it is written to an unborn child, "you". This child might read the poem when they are older.

Opening

The speaker begins by trying to answer a question, "what do you want/ A boy or a girl?" His answer "yes" annoys the people who are questioning him. They keep demanding an answer, which the poet doesn't give.

SOAPAIMS

This repetition suggests that the questioners are getting annoyed with the speaker, because he won't answer them in the way they want. They want him to prefer to have either a baby "boy" or "girl", and to prefer one sex more than the other. We can imagine these questioners might be his friends or his family.

Structure

The way the speaker keeps repeating "And I say" suggests that he is getting more and more angry that these people don't understand him.

Ending

Towards the end, he tries to make them understand him by using a metaphor, "we've stored up/ So much love/ It's spilling over everywhere." This suggests that the important thing to the speaker is the amount of "love" he and the mother are feeling for the unborn baby. This implies "love" is much more important than the baby's gender. It implies that the parents don't care what the baby's gender is.

The poem ends with the speaker speaking directly to the baby, "you". He wants the baby to know that their love is "spilling over everywhere." This suggests that the baby will be greeted with enormous amounts of love. It also implies that the parents are excited about the birth.

The final line changes the subject from "blue" or "pink" clothes, "I'm not sure/ There will be room for clothes." This suggests that love is much more important than the things, like clothes. Clothes are things they can buy the child, but it is love which will make them good parents.

312 words

Examiner's Comments

This answer is clearly structured, in paragraphs which follow the poem through from beginning to end.

The paragraphs follow a clear PEE structure, so each point is explained. The student uses 'suggests' and 'implies' to introduce the explanations.

There is a clear understanding of what the speaker wants to say, even though the student assumes that the speaker's voice is the same as the poet's voice.

It has a range of quotations.

It uses correct subject terminology, like metaphor and repetition.

The Unseen Comparison

You will be given a second poem which also appears pretty simple.

It will be on the same topic, so that even the sleepiest student will be able to spot something, anything, to compare!

Fit, by Dominic Salles

She tallies up

Your kicking

Out and in,

A hurricane of

Fists and feet and spin,

An iceberg hidden,

Floating under skin:

Now you're nearly out,

How will you fit in?

Question

In both 'Boy or Girl' and 'Fit' the speakers describe their attitudes to expecting a baby.

What are the similarities and/or differences between the ways the poets present these attitudes?

[8 marks]

The examiner is looking for only 4 things:

1. Any valid comparisons between the use of speaker's voice, perspective or **tone** to present **ideas and feelings**
2. Any valid comparisons between form **or structural features**
3. Any valid comparisons of **poetic techniques**, especially *metaphor, simile, alliteration, personification, sibilance*
4. Any valid comparisons between the choice of **vocabulary**, the semantic field and how this creates the **tone** of the speaker.

"Any valid comparison" means you notice any similarity or difference. Anything, it doesn't matter what, because that is the rule of the game.

This is because the examiners know the comparison is pretend English literature – it is just a skill that Ofqual has made them put in. *It makes getting the marks very easy though!*

Remember this is only 8 marks, so you only have about 12 minutes to answer it, and the examiners are not expecting much from you.

How to Compare

Simply, every time you make a point about the first poem, you then write how this is the similar or different to the other.

Then you say how that helps the persona in the poem share their point of view – in other words, you link it to the **tone.**

Tone is a sure way of getting top marks in this question.

Although the examiners would also like you to write about form, they realise that they will probably give you easy to understand, modern poems. Modern poems which won't have a form! So, you really, really need to earn this mark by writing about structure.

What is Structure?

You know that **contrast or juxtaposition, rhyme, repetition, half rhyme and free verse** are the go-to types of structure you will find in any poem. And of course the ending!

Always write about the *ending*, as it is always structure, and always suggests the poet's ideas and point of view.

So, you aren't going to worry about FOSSE way here. It's worth hardly any marks, just 8! So simply using and writing about two words, **structure** and **tone**, will make grade 7 highly likely, and grade 6 almost certain.

Exam Answer to Unseen Comparison

In 'Boy or Girl', the speaker's attitude is one of deep and overwhelming love for the unborn baby, so that love is "spilling over everywhere". However, in 'Fit' the speaker's **tone** is worried that the new baby might not "fit in" with the lifestyle of the parents.

Its **structure** has the repeated rhyme of "in, skin, spin." This lack of variety perhaps suggests that the new baby will also take the variety out of life as a parent. They will only be able to focus on the baby, nothing else.

This is reflected in the imagery describing the unborn baby as massive and threatening, so that the unborn baby is compared to both "a hurricane" and "an iceberg". These metaphors convey natural power, suggesting that the baby, though tiny, will be filled with a raw energy and power, like the "hurricane" which might destroy the speaker's life, as opposed to "fit in" to it. In addition, the baby as an "iceberg" conveys the speaker's fear about the unborn baby, which is hidden beneath the skin, presumably ready to sink his old life.

In contrast, the speaker in 'Boy or Girl' welcomes the "spilling" of love, and the implied mess of clothes "spilling". This lack of control over the future does not worry the speaker. The speaker welcomes uncertainty, not caring whether the baby is a "boy" or a "girl", allowing the baby to determine its own nature.

237 words – you could end here, as you have met all the marking criteria

However, in 'Fit', the speaker ends with a question apparently very worried about the effect of the new baby. The contrast of the tiny baby, with the much larger "hurricane" and "iceberg" implies that the speaker cannot imagine "how" the baby will "fit in" to his life, and will instead change it for the worse.

292 words – because I had some extra time – and I make sure I keep writing to the end.

Examiner Comments

Come on, you only have 12 minutes to write this answer, including reading the poem! I'm not going to expect much from you, just go through my checklist:

1. Did you compare – yes.
2. Did you comment on imagery – yes, metaphor.
3. Did you write about ideas and feelings – yes.
4. Did you cover a full range of ideas? – yes, you were able to because you wrote in PEE sentences.
5. Did you use the word 'tone'? – yes.
6. Did you specifically mention the structure of the poems? – Yes, you focused on the rhyme in one. You also explicitly wrote about the endings, explaining why the poems end the way they do. And you used the word 'structure".

Ok, have full marks!

Grade 6 Answer Unseen Comparison

Exam Answer

In 'Boy or Girl', the poet feels so much love for the unborn baby that love is "spilling everywhere". This is a metaphor which shows that this enormous amount of love can't even fit in the drawers.

In 'Fit' the poet doesn't mention love. The poet sounds worried that the new baby won't "fit in" to the old life of the parents. Maybe the poet doesn't really love the new baby yet, or is a bit worried that they won't love the baby.

Salles sees the baby as threatening. This is why the baby is described with the metaphors of "A hurricane" and "An iceberg". These suggest that the baby is dangerous, and might destroy their lives, because hurricanes and icebergs are both destructive.

'Boy or Girl' ends happily. Salles uses a metaphor that there might not be "room for clothes". This implies that there will be no "room" because there is so much love and nothing else can fit in.

'Fit' ends in a negative way. The question Salles asks is "How will you fit in?" Ending in this way suggests that he really believes the baby won't "fit in". This implies he is not looking forward to being a father.

202 Words

(Remember, I got grade 9 with only 237 words because I didn't write in PEE paragraphs)

Examiner Checklist:

1. Did you compare – yes.
2. Did you comment on imagery – yes, metaphor.
3. Did you write about ideas and feelings – yes, about feelings. No, about ideas.
4. Did you cover a full range of ideas? – no, all those PEE paragraphs meant it took a long time to deal with each idea.
5. Did you use the word 'tone'? – no, but you did write about the poet's feelings and attitude. You didn't consider that the poet and the speaker might have different views.
6. Did you specifically mention the structure of the poems? – not explicitly. Writing about the endings shows a clear understanding of structure, but you don't develop ideas about it.

Grade 6!

Leave it a couple of days, then try your own answer to the questions.

Compare them to these and see which one you are closer to, grade 6 or 9.

This section is not a bonus feature. It is fundamental. If you don't know these terms perfectly, you won't get a grade 7 or above.

Learn them!

Glossary of Terms

Simile: where you use the word "like" or "as" to make a comparison, describing why one thing is like another.

- His smile was *like* honey, sweet, alluring, promising a lifetime of plenty.
- The moment passed, *like* a rescue ship, and she was left alone, all alone, the sole survivor of the wreck of her marriage.
- The snake was *as* beautiful as a well told lie. It waited for the gullible dog.

Metaphor: where you make a comparison, by saying one thing is, or was something else.

- The moment passed, like a rescue ship, and she *was* left alone, all alone, *the sole survivor of the wreck of her marriage.*
- The music played *silver* notes, and the singers voice *was a diamond, a gift of love.*
- Summer *blazed in the wood,* colour *exploding up the tree trunks,* **licking the branches with warmth**.

Personification: where you use a simile or, more often, a metaphor to describe something that is not human, with characteristics which are human – like a person.

- The inscrutable police car sat motionless as a *judge weighing up* a death sentence.
- The sword *quivered with joy, ready* to punch, slash and stab.
- The TV *winked open* its giant eye, *inviting* me to get lost within.

Alliteration: where the **sounds** of consonants are the same in words that are close together. Usually, but not exclusively, the sounds will be at the beginning of words.

- *Creeping carefully*, the dog tra**ck**ed the scent of my **c**ooking, and *pounced* as I *poured* the gravy.
- "Forget the phone, you fool, it's *bugged*, and we're so *busted*."

- "It's not a party, it's a get together," complained Candace, while Phineas and Ferb laughed loud and long.

Sibilance: alliteration of the 'S' sound.

- The moment passed, like a rescue ship, and she was left alone, all alone, the sole survivor of the wreck of her marriage.
- Soft waves swept the shore, and the sand whispered like a waking lover.
- The pen scratched and scribbled, never stopping to make sense.

Onomatopoeia: words which recreate sounds. Usually they are spelt in such a way that they sound like the sounds they are describing. Note that alliteration can have an onomatopoeic effect.

- Soft waves swept the shore, and the sand whispered like a waking lover.
- The pen scratched and scribbled, never stopping to make sense.
- The sword quivered with joy, ready to punch, slash and stab.

Imagery: uses descriptive features like those listed above to recreate one or more of the senses. Don't just think of it as visual, but also sound, smell, taste, texture.

- The blue sky was bright with hope.
- The bed fought back, each lump in the mattress was a fist, both pillows slick with sweat like a boxer's chest.
- I stepped off the plane, tasted the heat of the sun, an exotic spice to the main course of my holiday to come.

Symbolism: something that stands for or represents something else, often an idea.

In **Little Red Riding Hood**, her name is symbolic of sexual experience, the Wolf is symbolic of male sexual desire which is portrayed as destructive. The mother's instruction to stay on the path is symbolic of following society's rules, and in particular preserving Little Red Riding Hood's virginity. The woodcutter who kills the wolf is symbolic of either the father's protection, or the finding of a true partner, depending on how you want to read the story. Now, you might not read the story this way at all, which is fine. However, you will need to provide your own symbolic interpretation – deal with the symbolism and you will ace grade 7 and beyond.

Contrast: two things that are put close together in order to emphasise the difference between them.

- The parental expectation that Jack is a useless son who has reduced them to poverty when selling their cow for beans, is contrasted with the resolution where the courageous, resourceful and lucky Jack raises the family to riches.

- The fate of the first two pigs, who built their houses quickly, is contrasted with the fate of the younger but wiser pig who builds his house of bricks.

- The warmth and promise of spring is contrasted with the melancholy and cold of winter.

Juxtaposition: two things that are put close together in order to emphasise the difference between them.

- "Give us a pound, mister," said the beggar, scrolling through the internet on his phone.

- The mother, tortured with pain, now smiled beatifically, while the baby, newly released, screamed incessantly.

- While the battle raged, the generals sat behind the front lines, drinking beers and stuffing three course meals.

Repetition: repeating a word, phrase, or idea. This can be done to emphasise, to create a rhythm or tone, or to reveal a contrast or comparison.

Register: In linguistics, a **register** is a variety of a language used for a particular purpose or in a particular setting.

What words give this the register of colloquial, American teenage language?

*"(Candace runs out to the **backyard**, she stares in shock upon seeing the rollercoaster, along with horror music)*

Candace: Phineas, what is this?!

Phineas: Do you like it?

Candace: Ooh, I'm gonna tell Mom, and when she sees what you're doing, **you are going down.** *(runs off)* **Down! Down! Down! D-O-W-N, down!"**

Which words deal with the idea of writing a novel?

"In my mind, I continually entertain myself with fragments of **narrative, dialogue** and **plot twists** but as soon as I'm in front of a **blank page**, they evaporate. I feel stuck. Sometimes I think I should give up, but I have convinced myself that if I can find a way to **write** more freely and suppress my inner critic, I could finally finish that **first draft**."

Allusion: is a brief and indirect reference to a person, place, thing or idea of historical, cultural, literary or political significance. It therefore depends on the reader being well read.

- Jose Mourinho attacks the game like a man who has been told that no man born of woman can ever defeat him. Unfortunately, it may be that Pep Guardiola was born by caesarean section. (Check out Macbeth for the allusion).
- Donald Trump loves ice cream. Forget Ben and Jerry's, he only likes Walls. (Ask a Mexican for the allusion)
- 2B or not 2B? Picasso picked up his pencil and wondered whether to paint or write a play. (You need to know something about Hamlet and the names of pencils for the allusions)

Reference: to mention or allude to something.

Synaesthesia: a figurative use of words that intends to draw out a response from readers stimulating more than one of the senses.

From **The Great Gatsby** by F. Scott Fitzgerald: "The lights grow brighter as the earth lurches away from the sun, and now the orchestra is playing yellow cocktail music, and the opera of voices pitches a higher key." Here the colour yellow invites us to imagine a happy sound to the music.

From Oscar Wilde's **An Ideal Husband**: "I believe they have got a mauve Hungarian band that plays mauve Hungarian music." The music sounds dull and tuneless, as mauve is a dull and muted form of purple.

In **Red,** by Taylor Swift, "Losing him was blue like I'd never known//Missing him was dark grey all alone." The colours reflect the singer's emotions. "Loving him was red." See – Little Red Riding Hood lives on!

You need to practise using all these words accurately. Then you need to practise memorizing them, so that you don't have to think about them – they need to be on the tip of your tongue, and on the tip of your pen in the exam.

Poetic Terminology

Alliteration

The repetition of stressed consonant sounds at the beginning of words within a phrase or verse line. Remember, 'phone' and 'family' uses alliteration, because of the consonant sounds: it doesn't have to be the same letter.

Anaphora

Often used in political speeches, anaphora is the repetition of a word or words at the beginning of successive phrases, clauses, or lines. **Checking Out Me History** and **The Charge of the Light Brigade** love this technique, which is a big clue that they are political poems.

Assonance

The repetition of vowel sounds without repeating consonants to create a mood. "The lone and level sands stretch far away" in Ozymandias uses the repeated sound of 'e' and 'a'.

Ballad

A popular narrative song. It usually uses (abcb) quatrains alternating four-stress and three-stress lines.

Blank verse

Unrhyming iambic pentameter. That means 10-syllables per line. It is the most common rhythm of traditional English dramatic and epic poetry, as it is considered the closest to English speech patterns. Robert Browning's dramatic monologues always use it.

Caesura

A stop or pause in a line, usually marked by some punctuation.

Consonance

The same as alliteration, except the consonant sounds can be anywhere in the word, not just at the beginning.

Couplet

A pair of successive rhyming lines, usually of the same length.

Dactyl

Three syllables where the first syllable is stressed, and the second and third are unstressed. Tennyson's **The Charge of the Light Brigade** is written in dactylic meter.

Dramatic monologue

A poem in which an imagined speaker addresses a silent listener, usually not the reader. Examples include Robert Browning's **My Last Duchess** and **Porphyria's Lover**.

End-stopped

A line ending with a punctuated stop, for example with a colon, a semicolon, exclamation mark or full stop.

Enjambment

The running-over of a sentence or phrase from one line of a poem to the next, without terminal punctuation; the opposite of end-stopped.

Meter

The rhythmical pattern of stressed and unstressed syllables in verse.

Metonymy

Substituting or replacing a thing with an associated part of the thing, for example calling someone a 'suit' instead of a businessman or business woman, business executive. Tennyson uses metonymy when replacing the Light Brigade with "noble six hundred".

Motif

A central or recurring image or action

Pastoral

Poets rejecting the modern, urban, industrial world and imagining a romantic ideal of life in a rural setting. Blake does this all the time, as does the Duchess in My Last Duchess.

Pathetic fallacy

Giving human feelings to inanimate objects, as coined by the Victorian literary critic John Ruskin. Nowadays, it is where anything in nature reflects the feelings of a character or narrator.

Pentameter

A line made up of five feet. It is the most common metrical line in English.

Persona

The speaker of the poem, who is not the poet, but a dramatic character.

Quatrain

A four-line stanza, with rhyme.

Refrain

A phrase or line repeated at intervals within a poem, especially at the end of a stanza.

Shakespearean sonnet

A sonnet made up of three quatrains and ending with a couplet, rhyming abab cdcd efef gg.

Sonnet

A 14 line poem coming from Italy and brought to England by Sir Thomas Wyatt and Henry Howard in the 16th century. It literally means "little song" and is nearly always a poem about love.

The Petrarchan sonnet has an eight-line stanza (octave) rhyming ABBAABBA, and a six-line stanza (sestet) rhyming CDCDCD or CDEEDE.

Stanza

A grouping of lines separated from others in a poem.

Synecdoche

A figure of speech in which a part of something stands for the whole, for example "all smiles stopped together" stands for the whole person being stopped, and in this example, killed.

Tone

The poet's attitude toward the poem's speaker, reader, and subject matter. It is the "mood" of the poem or persona. Tone is created by the poem's vocabulary, metre, rhyme, sound and imagery.

Trochee

The opposite of iambic. Here the first syllable is stressed, and the second syllable is unstressed.

Volta

It means 'trun' in Italian. It is where there is a sudden change of idea or point of view in a sonnet. In the Petrarchan sonnet it happens at the end of the octet, or the beginning of the sestet. Shelley uses it in Ozymandias. In a Shakespearian sonnet, it happens with the final couplet.

You will get away with calling any such turn a "volta" in any kind of poem.

Printed in Great Britain
by Amazon